THE ETHICAL AND POLITICAL

子 WORKS OF MOTSE 墨

THE ETHICAL AND POLITICAL WORKS
子 OF MOTSE 墨

TRANSLATED FROM THE ORIGINAL CHINESE TEXT

BY

YI-PAO MEI, Ph.D.

HYPERION PRESS, INC.
WESTPORT, CONNECTICUT

Library of Congress Cataloging in Publication Data

Mo, Ti, fl. 400 B. C.
   The ethical and political works of Motse.

   Reprint of the 1929 ed. published by A. Probsthain,
London, which was issued as v. 19 of Probsthain's
oriental series.
   Originally presented as the translator's thesis,
University of Chicago, 1927.
   I. Mei, Yi-pao, tr.   II. Title.
BL28.M6E5 1973   181'.11   73-893
ISBN 0-88355-085-7

Published in 1929
by Arthur Probsthain, London, England

First Hyperion reprint edition 1973

Library of Congress Catalogue Number 73-893

ISBN 0-88355-085-7

Printed in the United States of America

TABLE OF CONTENTS

CONTENTS

* indicates those chapters which are omitted in the present translation.

† indicates those chapters the text of which is lost.

PREFACE

Every civilization has its moulders and its spokesmen. While most recognized representatives of a culture have not been without their proper merit, many masterly and mighty souls have been allowed to sink into oblivion. In the case of China, Fate played her usual but tragic trick. While Confucius symbolizes to us the blooming flower of Chinese thought, Motse suggests but a faded blade. Yet what is, has not always been. At one time Moism with its forcefully stated doctrines on ethics, politics, economics, and religion seriously threatened Confucianism to become the representative Chinese view of life and way of living. As a matter of fact, Mencius tells us from his own mouth : " I am alarmed by these things and address myself to the defence of the doctrines of the former sages, and to oppose Yang (a follower of Taoism) and Mo." Unfortunately for the intellectual world, Confucianism finally won out through suppression of its rival systems, including Moism. As a formal discipline, Moism has been left little noticed through all these centuries, but as an habitual way of life it has taken deep root in the soil of the nation and the fibre of the people. The vitality of the philosophy is further evidenced by the fact that Young China in her present period of unrest is again eagerly turning to her old teacher who taught under rather similar conditions over two millenniums ago.

By way of introduction, we have to be contented with these few words just to bring out the historical position and the living significance of our author. The life of the teacher and the development of his school would constitute a fascinating romance, while the organization of his doctrines would make for a beautiful system. This thrilling task and pleasant duty we have tried to execute, and the results are embodied in a companion volume, *Motse, the Neglected Rival of Confucius*. Therefore further remarks could only be made at the risk of tedious repetition of what we have already put very simply there on the one hand, and of distracting the reader's attention from following the philosopher himself on the other.

A few explanations on the translation, however, may not be out of place. Sun Yi-Jang's *The Works of Motse with Commentaries* is universally adjudged the best among the Chinese texts of the *Works*. We have based our translation on his text and also our reading mainly on his commentaries. The few instances in which we have found it necessary to depart from his authority have been indicated in the footnotes.

The exclusion from the translation of the chapters in the *Works* that do not deal with ethical or political questions has been made both by choice and by necessity. As a glance at the " Table of Contents " will show, the chapters excluded belong to two groups, namely, the canonical chapters and their supplements and the chapters on military tactics. The latter group contain many obsolete terms and contribute little to make clear Motse's thought. Regarding the former group, besides the unsettled question as to their respective authorship, the few pages probably make the hardest reading in the whole body of Chinese literature. Even if one is sure of the meaning of their contents, which the present translator does not pretend to be, some other method than translation is necessary to convey the meaning intelligibly. As an excellent example we might cite Professor Hu Shih, who in his *The Development of the Logical Method in Ancient China*, attempted an exposition of some of the Motion canons.

The translation has been written quite independently. The result has been compared with the German translation of the complete *Works* by Professor Alfred Forke, which is the only other extensive translation of Motse in a European language. But on certain points, especially in his introductory essay, we have to disagree with his authority. At one stage in our investigation we tried to state the differences of opinion in their proper connexions, but later these notes appeared so laboured and suggestive of controversy that we decided to omit them altogether.

Regarding the English of the translation, we feel urged to repeat the explanation so often employed by translators. During the course of our work we have often had to face the dilemma between preserving the native colour and expression of the ancient Chinese author and employing modern idiomatic English. For evident reasons our decision has usually been for the former, sometimes, perhaps, at the expense of the latter. But we still hope we have succeeded in presenting the work in intelligible English.

The quotations from other works found in this volume are all translated from the respective Chinese texts. In the case of the numerous quotations from the Classics, we acknowledge the great pains taken by James Legge by giving reference to his translation of each passage, although we have very seldom been able to adopt his version without modification. This is done not only that the readers may be able to compare the different readings, but also that they may have the opportunity to get a view of the setting and significance of the passage where it is beyond the scope of the footnotes in this volume to make clear.

Besides my debt to Sun Yi-Jang as indicated above, I must take this opportunity to express my gratitude to Professor Lewis Hodous of Columbia University, who has patiently read over the MSS. in their first draft, and made numerous suggestions. I have taken advantage of a number of these. Dr. Berthold Laufer of the Chicago Field Museum has also spent time and given advice on the translation. To Professor J. H. Tufts of the University of Chicago, that high-minded and tender-hearted teacher, who not only gave constant encouragement throughout this undertaking but also spent his much needed vacation last Spring reading the MSS., I owe more than I can adequately express. Finally I want here to show my appreciation of the hospitality extended to me by the Library of Congress, Washington, D.C., where I did a large part of this translation under very favourable conditions.

Y. P. Mei.

London.

July, 1927.

BOOK I

CHAPTER I [1]

Befriending the Learned [2]

If one does not preserve the learned in a state he will be injuring the state ; if one is not zealous (to recommend) the virtuous upon seeing one, he will be neglecting the ruler. Enthusiasm is to be shown only to the virtuous, and plans for the country are only to be shared with the learned. Few are those, who, neglecting the virtuous and slighting the learned, could still maintain the existence of their countries.

Formerly Lord Wen (of Chin 780–746 B.C.[3]) was once in exile and yet later became the leading feudal lord. Lord Huan (of Ch'i 685–643 B.C.) was once forced to leave his state and yet later became a "tyrant" [4] among the feudal lords. Lord Kou Chien of Yüeh (496–465 B.C.) was once brought under humiliation by the king of Wu [5], and yet he was later

---

[1] This and the two following chapters are judged to be spurious almost unanimously by competent textual critics. The content of this chapter is nothing more than an appendix to the three synoptic chapters VIII–X on " Exaltation of the Virtuous ", and should not, therefore, occupy the position of the opening chapter in the book.

[2] The English word " learned " is no equivalent to the Chinese word shih 士, as virtue, talent, and courage are to be embodied by the shih as well as learning. He is really a philosopher-gentleman of the noblesse of the sword.

[3] All dates so inserted indicate the period of the reign of the ruler.

[4] " Tyrant " 霸 is here used in the Greek sense. See the Chronological Table appended in the companion volume, *Motse, the Neglected Rival of Confucius*.

[5] The reference here is to Lord Fu Ch'a of Wu, 495–473 B.C.

looked upon with awe by the princes of China.[1] The reason
that these three men became famous and successful in the
world lies in that they were able to endure shame and humiliation within their states.

The greatest men know of no defeat. The next greatest
turn failure into success, and this, by the employment of
the people.

I have heard it said : It is not that there is no peaceful
abode but that I have no peaceful heart (over others' home-
lessness) ; it is not that my wealth is not sufficient but that
my passion yearns for more (to improve others' conditions).
Therefore the superior man is strict with one's self but lenient
with others (in matters of conduct) while the multitude
are lenient with themselves but strict with others. The
superior man carries out his ambitions successfully in action
and studies the situation when he is at leisure. Even when
he is taken as a mediocre individual he feels no dissatisfaction.
This is because he has self-confidence. Therefore, those who
attempt what seems difficult to them will obtain what they
desire, but few who aim at what they desire can avoid what
they dislike.[2]

Therefore, artful ministers are harmful to the lord and
flattering subordinates are injurious to the ruler. The lord
should have uncompromising ministers ; the ruler should
have stern subordinates. Only when counsel is given with
far-sightedness and advice administered with sternness,

---

[1] Yüeh was on the southern border of China. It was barbarian in
origin too.   Cf. the Sketch Map appended in *Motse, the Neglected Rival
of Confucius.*

[2] This is almost an anticipation of the modern criticism of the Hedonistic
Paradox.

can the life of the state be secure and permanent. If (to the contrary) the subordinates should value their positions and keep silence, the ministers near at hand would be speechless and those far away could only sigh, and the people would become bitter. When the ruler is surrounded with praises and flatteries and insulated against good counsels, then the country is in danger. Was it not because they would not employ the scholars, that Chieh [1] and Chow [2] lost their empire and their lives ? Thus it is said : To offer the greatest treasure of the country to the ruler is not as laudable as to recommend the virtuous and introduce the learned.

Among the five weapons the sharpest will be broken first. Among the five swords the keenest will be first worn out. The sweet wells become sooner dry and the elegant trees are oftener felled. The tortoises that are more responsive are oftener burned and the snakes that show more magic power are more sacrificed. Thus, Pi Kan [3] died of his uprightness ; Meng Fen [4] perished by his strength ; Hsi Shih [5]

---

[1] Chieh was the last king of Hsia Dynasty, 1818–1766 B.C.

[2] Chow was the last king of Shang Dynasty, 1154–1122 B.C.

[3] Pi Kan was a royal uncle of the wicked King Chow. He was so daring in his counsels that Chow tortured him to death.

[4] Meng Fen was a man of great strength. He was said to have plucked the horns out of oxen's heads. But, chronologically, he belongs to the end of the fourth century B.C., and Motse could not be still living to know him. The ready explanation is that this incident was inserted by a later writer. But, as was pointed out in the note at the beginning of this chapter, the text of this and the next two chapters has been so much tampered with that it is hardly worth the effort to try to account for every incongruity.

[5] Hsi Shih was a famous beauty of the fifth century B.C. Lord Kou Chien of Yüeh made a present of her to Lord Fu Ch'a of Wu who were military rivals. Fu Ch'a could not resist her charms and Wu dissipated. Wu was soon after absorbed by Yüeh.

paid with her life for her beauty ; and Wu Ch'i [1] was torn
alive for his achievement. This shows that there are but
few who excel other people and do not perish on account
of it. Hence the saying : Position of the supreme is hard
to keep.

Even the kind ruler will not show favours to ministers
without merit. Even the affectionate father will not love
his useless sons. He who occupies a position but is not
equal to the task is not the proper person for the position.
He who draws emoluments but does not deserve the rank is
not the proper proprietor of the emoluments. Good bows
may be hard to draw, but they can reach great heights and
pierce deeply. Good horses may be hard to ride on, but
they can carry heavy burdens and make long journeys.
Real talents may be hard to command, but they can be
trusted to be envoys to the court of the emperor and to meet
the nobility.

Therefore the big rivers do not despise the little brooklets
for tributaries. And great men do not neglect any menial
task or reject any trifle, and so they become vessels for the
world. The water in a river does not come from a single
source, neither is the fur coat that is worth a thousand yi [2]

---

[1] Wu Ch'i was a great general of the State of Ch'u, one of the most feared
military men of the period. King Tao, the reigning ruler of Ch'u and master
of Wu Ch'i, died in 381 B.C. Wu Ch'i was thereupon cruelly put to death
by his fellow ministers, who had been envying his glory and honour. It is
quite doubtful, however, whether Motse could have lived to see this event.
See the discussion on the dates of Motse in *Motse, the Neglected Rival of
Confucius*, chap. ii.

[2] Yi 鎰 is an ancient measure of silver. It is sometimes given as
equivalent to 20 taels and sometimes as 24.

composed of the white fur [1] of a single fox. Now, to discard
those who agree with the right but employ those who agree
with one's self is not the way to be a great ruler. (Just
as) Heaven and earth do not dazzle, great bodies of water
do not boil and foam, and great conflagrations do not coruscate,
(so) the imperial character does not lift itself up beyond
reach.

As to the chieftain of only a thousand people, he is straight
like an arrow and smooth like a hone, unable to tolerate the
manifold ways. For narrow gorges dry up rapidly, shallow
streams are soon exhausted, and the barren land does not
bear fruits. When a ruler confines his favours within his
palace, then they cannot be shared by the whole country.

---

[1] This is the part of the fur of the fox that comes from under its legs.
It is both light and warm.

CHAPTER II

Self-Cultivation

Though there should be tactics in war, courage is fundamental. Though there should be ceremonies for mourning, grief is essential. Though a scholar should be learned, he must first of all exhibit good conduct. When the seeds are not well sown, there is no use in labouring for a good harvest. When the people near-by are not befriended there is no use of endeavouring to attract those at a distance. When one's relatives are not submissive, there is no use in endeavouring to establish contacts with the outside world. When one cannot accomplish a single task from beginning to end, there is no use of attempting many things. And when one is ignorant of a commonplace that is pointed out, there is no use of pursuing wide knowledge.

Therefore, when the early kings administered the empire, they would investigate what was within reach and attract those at a distance. Investigation of a locality by the superior men means its orderly government. When they discovered misconduct or depravity, they corrected themselves. Thus all complaints disappeared and conduct became regulated (by itself). When the superior men do not listen to treacherous words or utter any threatening sound, or entertain any idea of injuring somebody, then even if there were underhanded persons they would lose support. Therefore the superior men are daily more energetic in performing their duty, but weaker in their desires, and more stately in their appearance.

The way of the superior man makes the individual incorruptible in poverty and righteous when wealthy; it makes him love the living and mourn the dead. These four qualities of conduct cannot be hypocritically embodied in one's personality. There is nothing in his mind that goes beyond love; there is nothing in his behaviour that goes beyond respectfulness, and there is nothing from his mouth that goes beyond gentility. When one pursues such a way until it pervades his four limbs and permeates his flesh and skin, and until he becomes white-haired and bald-headed without ceasing, one is truly a sage.

His wisdom will not be far-reaching whose purpose is not firm. His action will not be effective whose promises are not kept. He who will not share his possessions with others is not worthy to be a friend. And he who does not stand firm on principles and has neither wide knowledge nor penetrating judgment, is not worthy to be a companion. Just as a weak trunk will have but small branches, so, mere bravery without cultivation will result in dissipation. And just as a dirty source will issue in an impure stream, so unfaithful conduct will unfavourably affect one's fame. For, fame does not spring up out of nothing, nor does praise grow by itself. Fame follows upon success and is not obtainable by hypocrisy.

He will not be listened to who talks much but is slow in action, even though he is discerning. He will not accomplish anything who is capable but likes to boast of his feats, even though he drudges. The wise discerns all in his mind but speaks simply, and he is capable but does not boast of his deeds. And, so, his name is exalted the world over. In speech, not quantity but ingenuity, not eloquence but insight, should be cultivated. If one is not wise and without insight, breeding only dissipation in one's personality, this is just the contrary of what should be cultivated.

Any virtue that does not spring from the heart will not remain and any (result of) action that is not aimed at by one's self will not stay. There is no short cut to fame and there is no trick to praise. The superior man regards his body but as the vehicle for his character. None who places much importance on personal gains but lightly sacrifices his fame has ever become a gentleman in the world.

CHAPTER III

On Dyeing [1]

Watching a dyer of silk at work, Motse sighed, saying : What is dyed in blue becomes blue, what is dyed in yellow becomes yellow. When the silk is put in a different dye, its colour becomes also different. Having been dipped in five times, it has changed its colour five times. Therefore dyeing should be done with great care. This is true not only with silk dyeing ; even a country changes its colour in response to its influences.[2]

Thus Shun came under the influences of Hsü Yu [3] and Po Yang [3] ; Yü, under that of Kao T'ao [3] and Po Yi [3] ; T'ang, under that of Yi Yin [3] and Chung Huei [3] ; and King Wu, under that of the Grand Duke [3] and Duke Chou.[3] Now these four kings had been under good influences. Therefore they came to possess the empire and were commissioned Sons of Heaven (Emperors).[4] Their achievements and great fame extended from Heaven to earth. And when the pre-eminently magnanimous and righteous figures of the world are mentioned, they are invariably those referred to.

[1] Many historical figures cited in this chapter lived long after the time of Motse. All that can be attributed to Motse in this chapter is that watching some dyer at work he was impressed by the powerfulness of the dyes.

[2] There is a pun in the Chinese word jan 染. It means, among other things, to dye and also to influence.

[3] These are the noted virtuous men in ancient Chinese history.

[4] In Chinese the same term T'ien Tse, 天 子, literally Son of Heaven, means also the Emperor. The former gives the religious while the latter the political emphasis. This double character of the term also expresses the Chinese political idea of the government as a trust from Heaven.

Chieh of Hsia came under the influence of Kan Hsin[1] and T'uei Yi[1] ; Chow of Yin, under that of the Duke of Ch'ung[1] and E Lai[1] ; King Li, under that of Ch'ang Fu, Duke Li[1], and Yi Chung of the State of Jung[1] ; and King Yu, under that of Yi, Duke of Fu,[1] and Ku, Duke of Ts'ai.[1] Now these four kings had been under bad influences. Therefore they lost their empire and their lives, and were persecuted everywhere. And when the most unrighteous and shameful persons of the world are mentioned, they are invariably those referred to.

Lord Huan of Ch'i came under the influence of Kuan Chung[2] and Pao Shu[2] ; Lord Wen of Chin, under that of Uncle Fan[2] and Kao Yen[2] ; Lord Chuang of Ch'u, under that of Sun Shu[2] and the Minister of Shen[2] ; Ho Lü of Wu, under that of Wu Yuan[2] and Wen Yi[2] ; and Kou Chien of Yüeh, under that of Fan Li[2] and Minister Chung.[2] Now these five lords had been under good influences. Therefore they became Tyrants[3] among the feudal lords and their achievements and their fame were handed down to posterity.

Fan Chi She came under the influence of Ch'ang Liu Shuo[4] and Wang Sheng[4] ; Chung Hsing Yin, under that of Chi Ch'in[4] and Kao Chiang[4] ; Fu Ch'a, under that of Wang Sun Lo[4] and Minister P'i[4] ; Chih Po Yao, under that of

---

[1] These are the noted wicked men in ancient Chinese history, assistants of the wicked kings and accomplices with them in sin and cruelty.

[2] These are the able assistants to the great feudal lords of the period, who are instrumental to the latter's success.

[3] The word is used in the Greek sense. A comparison with the list of the Five Tyrants in the Chronological Table appended in *Motse, the Neglected Rival of Confucius* will show that the use of the word here is not historically strict.

[4] These are the wicked helpers of the unsuccessful princes.

Chih Kuo [1] and Chang Wu [1] ; Shang of Chung Shan, under that of Wei Yi [1] and Yen Ch'ang [1] ; and Lord K'ang of Sung, under that of T'ang Yang [1] and T'ien Pu Li.[1] Now, these six princes had been under bad influences. Therefore their states were ruined and they were executed, their ancestral temples were destroyed and descendants annihilated. The rulers and the subjects were dispersed and the people were left homeless. The whole world point to these six princes as the most greedy and disturbing people.

Now, how can the rulers obtain security ? They can obtain it by following the right way. And one will naturally follow the right way when under good influence. Therefore capable rulers are very painstaking in the selection of men while they may not be so careful in attending to the administration (themselves). But the incapable wear out their body and exhaust their energy, tax their mind and stretch their thought, and yet their states are only placed in greater danger and their persons under more humiliation. Now, it is not that these six princes do not value their states or hold their lives cheap, it is really that they do not understand the relative importance of things. And it is due to bad influences that their idea of importance is distorted.

Not only states but also individuals are subject to influences. If one has for friends none but those who love magnanimity and righteousness and who are careful and respectful of course one's family will become more prosperous, one's person more at peace, and one's name more honourable every day ; and, as an official, one will be properly qualified.

---

[1] These are the wicked helpers of the unsuccessful princes.

Examples of such are Tuan Kan Mu,[1] Ch'intse,[2] and Fu Yüeh.[3] (On the contrary) if one has for friends none but those who are proud and quarrelsome and who pretend to be intimate, naturally one's family will be reduced to straits, one's person will be more in danger, and one's name more dishonourable every day and one will not be qualified for office. And, examples of such are Tse Hsi, Yi Ya, and Shu Tiao.

An Ode[4] says: " One must choose what to be tinged with." To be careful about what one is to be tinged with is just the theme of this (essay).

---

[1] Tuan Kan Mu was a pupil of Tse Hsia, who was a noted disciple of Confucius.

[2] Ch'intse was a disciple of Motse. *Infra*, pp. 218 and 259.

[3] Fu Yüeh is a great virtuous man. For full story see p. 43, note 3.

[4] This must be a lost ode.

CHAPTER IV [1]

ON THE NECESSITY OF STANDARDS

Motse said : To accomplish anything whatsoever one must have standards. None has yet accomplished anything without them. The gentlemen fulfilling their duties as generals and councillors have their standards. Even the artisans performing their tasks also have their standards. The artisans make square objects according to the square, circular objects according to the compasses ; they draw straight lines with the carpenter's line and find the perpendicular by a pendulum. All artisans, whether skilled or unskilled, employ these five [2] standards. Only, the skilled workers are accurate. Though the unskilled labourers have not attained accuracy, yet they do better by following these standards than otherwise. Thus all artisans follow the standards in their work.

Now, the government of the empire and that of the large states do not observe their standards. This shows the governors are even less intelligent than the artisans.

What, then, should be taken as the proper standard in government ? How will it do for everybody to imitate [3]

---

[1] This chapter seems to be an appendix or summary of the central themes in chapters xiv–xvi on "UNIVERSAL LOVE" and chapters xxvi–viii on "WILL OF HEVAEN".

[2] Only four are mentioned above. In the "K'AO KUNG CHI" in *Chou Li,* 周 禮 考 工 記 or *Manual on Crafts*, a fifth standard is specified which is somehow here omitted, namely " find the level with water ".

[3] Here in Chinese the same word for " standard " 法 is used. The more literal translation will be " take as standard ". But as it will be often repeated in the subsequent text, this is too clumsy.

his parents ? There are numerous parents in the world but few are magnanimous. For everybody to imitate his parents is to imitate the unmagnanimous. Imitating the unmagnanimous can not be said to be following the proper standard. How will it do for everybody to follow his teacher ? There are numerous teachers in the world but few are magnanimous. For everybody to imitate his teacher is to imitate the unmagnanimous. Imitating the un-magnanimous cannot be taken as following the proper standard. How will it do for everybody to imitate his ruler ? There are many rulers in the world but few are magnanimous. For everybody to imitate the ruler is to imitate the unmagnanimous. Imitating the unmagnanimous cannot be taken as following the right standard. So then neither the parents nor the teacher nor the ruler should be accepted as the standard in government.

What then should be taken as the standard in government ? Nothing better than following Heaven. Heaven is all-inclusive and impartial in its activities, abundant and unceasing in its blessings, and lasting and untiring in its guidance. And, so, when the sage-kings had accepted Heaven as their standard, they measured every action and enterprise by Heaven. What Heaven desired they would carry out, what Heaven abominated they refrained from.

Now, what is it that Heaven desires, and what that it abominates ? Certainly Heaven desires to have men benefit and love one another and abominates to have them hate and harm one another. How do we know that Heaven desires to have men love and benefit one another and abominates to have them hate and harm one another ? Because it

loves and benefits men universally. How do we know that
it loves and benefits men universally ? Because it claims
all and accepts offerings from all.   All states in the world,
large or small, are cities of Heaven, and all people, young
or old, honourable or humble, are its subjects ; for they
all graze oxen and sheep, feed dogs and pigs, and prepare
clean wine and cakes [1] to sacrifice to Heaven. Does this
not mean that Heaven claims all and accepts offerings from
all ?   Since Heaven does claim all and accepts offerings from
all, what then can make us say that it does not desire men
to love and benefit one another ?   Hence those who love and
benefit others Heaven will bless.   Those who hate and harm
others Heaven will curse, for it is said that he who murders
the innocent will be visited by misfortune.   How else can
we explain the fact that men, murdering each other, will be
cursed by Heaven ?   Thus we are certain that Heaven
desires to have men love and benefit one another and
abominates to have them hate and harm one another.

The ancient sage-kings, Yü, T'ang, Wen, and Wu [2] loved
the people of the world universally, leading them to reverence
Heaven and worship the spirits. Many were their benefits
to the people. And, thereupon Heaven blessed them,
establishing them emperors ; and all the feudal lords of the
empire showed them respect.   (On the other hand) the wicked

---

[1] These sacrificial cakes are to be of a particular description, namely,
to be made of millet and glutinous rice.

[2] These are the famous sage-kings of the Three Dynasties, namely,
Hsia, Shang, and Chou. See the Chronological Table appended in *Motse,
the Neglected Rival of Confucius,* for their dates and historical setting.

kings, Chieh, Chow, Yu, and Li,[1] hated all the people in the world, seducing the people to curse Heaven and ridicule the spirits. Great were their injuries to the people. Thereupon Heaven brought them calamity, depriving them of their empire and their lives; and posterity condemned them to this day. Chieh, Chow, Yu, and Li, then, are those that committed evil and were visited by calamities. And, Yü, T'ang, Wen, and Wu are those that loved and benefited the people and obtained blessings. Thus we have those who obtained blessings because they loved and benefited the people as well as those who were visited by calamities because they hated and harmed the people.

[1] These wicked men were the descendants of the sage-kings, Yü, T'ang, Wen, and Wu respectively, and the last kings of the Three Dynasties just as the latter were the first kings of them. See Chronological Table referred to in the last footnote.

CHAPTER V [1]

THE SEVEN CAUSES OF ANXIETY

Motse said : There are seven causes of worry to a state and they are : (1) When the outer and the inner city walls are not defensible; (2) When an enemy state is approaching and yet one's neighbours do not come to the rescue; (3) When the resources of the people have all been spent on useless enterprises and gifts all squandered upon incapable men, when people's resources are exhausted without producing any profit and the treasury is emptied by entertaining idle company; (4) When the officials value only their salaries, and the sophists [2] only friendship, and when the subordinates dare not remonstrate against the laws the ruler has made for persecution; (5) When the lord is over-confident of his own wisdom and holds no consultation, when he feels he is secure and makes no preparations against attack, and when he does not know that he must be watchful while neighbours are planning against him; (6) When those trusted are not loyal and the loyal are not trusted; and (7) When the crops are not sufficient for food and the ministers can not be charged with responsibilities, and when awards fail to make people happy and punishment to make them afraid. With these seven causes present in the maintenance of the state, the

---

[1] This and the next chapters seem to be supplements to chapters xx-xxii, on "ECONOMY OF EXPENDITURES".

[2] There is some remarkable similarity between the Greek sophist and the Chinese yu k'o, 游 客. In both cases they started to be travelling teachers of wisdom, including the art of rhetoric and statecraft, but degenerated into jugglers of words or even worse. Cf. *Motse, the Neglected Rival of Confucius*, chap. i.

state will perish, and, in the defence of a city, the city will be reduced to ruin by the approaching enemy. Wherever these seven causes are found, the country will face calamity.

Now, the five grains [1] are the people's mainstay and the source of the ruler's revenue. When the people lose their support the ruler cannot have any revenue either. And without food the people will not observe order. Therefore, food should be secured, land cultivated and expenditures cut down. When all the five grains are gathered, all the five tastes [2] will be offered the ruler ; when not all gathered, the five tastes will not be all offered.

Failure of one grain is called dearth 饉 ; failure of two grains is called scarcity 罕 ; failure of three grains is called calamity 凶 ; failure of four grains is called want 餽 ; and failure of all five grains is called famine 饑. When the country is in dearth, all the salaries of the officials below the rank of the minister will be reduced by one-fifth ; in scarcity, they will be reduced by two-fifths ; in calamity, they will be reduced by three-fifths ; in want, they will be reduced by four-fifths ; and when famine is in the country there will be no salaries beyond their rations. Therefore when famine and dearth visit a country, the ruler will omit three from the five items of sacrifice, the officials will suspend the courts, and the scholars will not go to school and the lord will not put on his robe to give audience. Even envoys from other

---

[1] The five grains are : (1) rice, (2) millet, (3) millet of a different variety, (4) wheat, and (5) soy beans.

[2] The five tastes include bitter, hot, sour, sweet, and salty. But ordinarily it is used figuratively, signifying elaborate cooking and sumptuous food.

feudal lords and messengers from neighbouring states are entertained with cooked food only, and it is not sumptuous. The side-horses of the carriage-team are done away with and the walks (in the palace) are not weeded. Neither are the horses fed with grains, nor are the concubines and maids clothed with silk. And this is the sign of extreme scarcity.

Now, if carrying her child and drawing water from a well, a woman dropped the child into the well, she would of course endeavour to get it out. But famine and dearth is a much greater calamity than the dropping of a child. Should there not be also endeavour (to prevent it)? People are gentle and kind when the year is good, but selfish and vicious when it is bad. Yet, how can they be held responsible? When many produce but few consume then there can be no bad year; on the contrary, when few produce but many consume then there can be no good year. Thus it is said: scarcity of supply should stimulate study of the seasons and want of food demands economy of expenditures.

The ancients produced wealth according to seasons. They ascertained the source of wealth before they appropriated the products, and therefore they had plenty. Could even the ancient sage-kings cause the five grains invariably to ripen and be harvested and the floods and the droughts never to occur? Yet, none were frozen or starved, why was it? It was because they made full use of the seasons and were frugal in their own maintenance. The history of Hsia says that the Deluge lasted seven years in the time of Yü and the history of Yin[1] tells that a drought visited

---

[1] Yin is a second name for the Dynasty of Shang. Cf. *Motse, the Neglected Rival of Confucius*, chap. i.

T'ang for five years. These are the extremes of disasters. Yet the people were not frozen or starved. Why was this so ? The reason lies in diligent production and thrifty consumption. Therefore, famine and dearth cannot be prepared against unless there are stored grains in the granaries, and justice cannot be maintained against the unjust unless there are ready weapons in the armoury. One cannot defend himself unless the inner and the outer city walls are in repair, and one cannot meet emergencies unless his ideas are well thought out. Thus Ch'ing Chi[1] was unprepared, and he should not have set out on the journey. Chieh made no preparations against T'ang and he was sent to exile. And Chow made no preparations against Wu and he was executed. Now, Chieh and Chow were both emperors in rank and possessed the whole empire, yet they both perished at the hands of rulers (of states) of only a hundred li[2] square. What is the reason for this ? Because they depended on their rank and wealth and made no preparations. Therefore, preparation is what a country should emphasize. Supply is the treasure of a country, armament its claws, and the city walls are the stronghold of its self-defence. And these three items are the essentials to the existence of a state.

(The present rulers) squander great amounts of wealth to reward the undeserving, empty the treasury to acquire carriages and horses, exhaust the labourers to build palaces and furnish amusements. Upon their death, again, thick coffins and many coats and fur coats are to be furnished.

---

[1] Ch'ing Chi was a powerful man in the state of Wu. He was induced to take the journey here referred to and was murdered on the way.

[2] A li 里 is equal to approximately ⅓ mile.

Porches and pavilions are built for them while they are living, and tombs when they are dead. By this the people are embittered and the treasury is left lean. While the amusements are not yet satisfying to the superiors, the hardship already becomes unbearable for the subjects. Such a state will fall under any attack and such people will perish by famine. And all this is due to the absence of preparation. Moreover, food is what the sages treasured. The history of Chou says : " Without three years' food (in store) a state cannot be a state (as it is in danger of losing its sovereignty). A family being without food in store to be sufficient for three years its children cannot be its children (who are in danger of being abandoned or sold to others)." Such, then, is the preparation of a country.

CHAPTER VI

INDULGENCE IN EXCESS

Motse said : Before the art of building houses and palaces
was known primitive people lingered by the mounds and
lived in caves. It was damp and injurious to health. Thereupon the sage-kings [1] built houses and palaces. The guiding
principles for these buildings were these : The house shall
be built high enough to avoid the damp and moisture ; the
walls thick enough to keep out the wind and cold ; the roof
strong enough to stand snow, frost, rain, and dew ; and the
walls in the palace high enough to observe the propriety of
the sexes. These are sufficient, and any expenditure of
money and energy that does not bring additional utility shall
not be permitted. When the city walls are repaired with
regular labour, the people may feel tired but there is no
exhaustion. When taxes are collected according to custom,
the people may be deprived of some money but there is no
bitterness. The real woe of the people does not lie here,
it lies in heavy taxes.

The sage-kings built houses and palaces in order to better
the living conditions and not for pleasures of sight. They
made clothes and hats, belts and shoes in order to protect
the body and not for novelty. They were thrifty themselves
and taught the people to be the same. And, so, the people
in the whole world became orderly and wealth was sufficient

---

[1] The " sage-kings " here seem to refer to the Nest Builders. They have
always been regarded as the first teachers of the art of house building.
They lived in the fourth millennium B.C. Cf. *Motse, the Neglected Rival of
Confucius*, chap. i.

for use. When the present rulers build their residences, they are quite different from this. They would heavily tax the people, robbing them of their means of livelihood, in order to have their palaces covered with porches and pavilions in various designs and adorned with paintings and sculpture. When the ruler builds his palaces in this fashion, his assistants naturally imitate him. And, so, there is not sufficient wealth to prepare against famine and dearth or to relieve the orphans and widows. And the people become more unruly as the state becomes poorer. If the rulers sincerely desire to have the empire orderly and hate to see it in disorder, they must not indulge in building houses and palaces.

Before clothing was known the primitive people wore coats of furs and belts of straw. They were neither light and warm in winter nor light and cool in summer. The sage-king [1] thought this did not satisfy the needs of man. So, he taught the women to produce silk and flax and to weave cloth and linen, therewith to make clothing for the people. The guiding principles for clothing were these : In winter the underwear shall be made of spun-silk so as to be light and warm. In summer it shall be made of coarse flax so as to be light and cool. And this is sufficient. Therefore the sages made their clothes just to fit their stature and size, and not for the purpose of pleasing the senses or to dazzle the common people. In that age, durable carts and gentle horses were not valued, neither were sculpture and adornments prized. What is the reason for this ? The reason lies in

---

[1] This seems to refer to Huang Ti, 2697–2597 B.C., whose consort first taught the women the art of raising silk-worms. Cf. *Motse, the Neglected Rival of Confucius*, chap. i.

the kind of leadership. The people had sufficient means
of livelihood in their home to meet either drought or flood,
dearth or famine, Why ? Because they understood the
needs of self-support and paid little attention to external
appearance. So, the people were frugal and orderly and the
ruler was thrifty and easily supported. The store house
and treasury were full, prepared against misfortunes. Armour
and weapons were not left in disuse and the soldiers and the
people were not tired, ready to punish the unsubmissive.
Thus the ruler could become a tyrant over the empire.

The present rulers are quite different from this when
they make their clothes. Having what is warm and light in
winter and what is light and cool in summer, they would yet
heavily tax the people, robbing them of their means of livelihood, in order to have elaborately embroidered and gorgeous
garments. Hooks are made of gold and ornaments on the
girdle consist of pearls and jades. Women are employed
to make the embroidery and men to do the carving. All
these are for the adornment of the body. They really add
little to its warmth. Wealth is squandered and energy
wasted all for naught. So, then, when clothing is made
not for the body but for brilliant appearance, the people
will be wicked and unruly and the ruler extravagant and
deaf to good counsel. It will be impossible to keep the country
out of disorder. If the rulers sincerely desire the empire
to have order and hate to see it in disorder, they must not
indulge in making clothing excessively.

Before the art of cooking was known, primitive people ate
only vegetables and lived in separation. Thereupon the sage [1]

---

[1] This seems to refer to Shen Nung, twenty-eighth century B.C., the father
of Chinese agriculture and medicine. Cf. *Motse, the Neglected Rival of
Confucius*, chap. i.

taught the men to attend to farming and to plant trees to supply the people with food. And the sole purpose of securing food is to increase energy, satisfy hunger, strengthen the body and appease the stomach. He was frugal in spending wealth and simple in habits of living, and, so, the people became rich and the country orderly.

With the present rulers all is different. They would heavily tax the people in order to enjoy elaborately the different meats and fish and turtle cooked in various ways. (The lord of) a large state is served with a hundred courses and (that of) a small state, with tens of courses, which will cover a table space of ten square feet. The eyes cannot see all the dishes, the hands cannot handle them all, and the mouth cannot taste them all. In winter they will freeze, and in summer they sour. As the ruler serves himself thus, naturally his assistants imitate him. And so the rich and high in rank are wasteful and extravagant, while the solitary and miserable are hungry and cold. It is impossible to keep such a state out of disorder. If the rulers sincerely desire the empire to have order and hate to see it in disorder, they must not indulge in excessive eating and drinking.

Before the primitive people knew how to make boats and carts they could neither carry a heavy load nor travel a great distance. Thereupon the sage-king [1] made boats and carts to facilitate the people. The boats and carts were made durable and convenient so that they would carry much and travel far. Such an undertaking takes little wealth but produces many benefits. Naturally the people found

---

[1] This seems also to refer to Huang Ti, to whom the invention of boat and vehicle is traditionally ascribed.

it agreeable and convenient. The people were not tired
out and yet the ruler's needs were all supplied. So, people
were attracted to him.

When the present rulers make boats and carts, it is quite
different. Having made them durable and convenient,
they would yet heavily tax the people to decorate them.
The carts are decorated with embroidery and boats with
carving. Women have to stop weaving to do the embroidery
so the people are left cold. While men have to abandon
agriculture to do the carving and so the people become hungry.
When the ruler builds such boats and carts for himself,
naturally his assistants imitate him. Therefore the people
become victims of both hunger and cold, and they commit
wickedness. Much wickedness is followed by heavy punishment, and heavy punishment places the country in disorder.
If the rulers sincerely desire the empire to have order and
hate to see it in disorder, they must not indulge themselves
in constructing boats and carts excessively.

Every creature living between Heaven and earth and within
the four seas [1] partakes of the nature of Heaven and earth
and the harmony of the Yin and the Yang.[2] Even the
greatest sages cannot alter this. How do we know ? When
they taught about Heaven and earth, they dwelt on the upper
and the lower spheres and the four seasons, the principles
of Yin and Yang and human nature, the phenomena of men

---

[1] This is the primitive Chinese conception of the world. It has been
made famous by the often quoted Confucian saying : " Within the four
seas all are brothers."

[2] This harmony is one of two principles in constant strife against each
other. Compare this metaphysical concept of reality with the Pythagorean
ἁρμονίη and the Herakleitean " opposite tension ".

and women, birds and animals, and that of the sexes. Even the early kings could not escape from the fundamentals of nature. Even the great sages of ancient times must keep a household.[1] Only, as their conduct was not unfavourably affected, there was no dissatisfaction among the people, and as women were not kept within the palace (to be spinsters) there were few bachelors in the empire. As women were not kept within the palace and as there were few bachelors abroad, the population in the empire was large.

The present rulers of large states retain as many women as a thousand in their household and those of small states as many as a hundred. Therefore men in the empire are mostly without wife and women without husband. The functions of men and women are prevented and the population becomes small. If the rulers sincerely desire the population to be large and hate to see it small, they must not indulge in retaining too many women.

Now, in these five things[2] the sages are temperate and economical while the wicked men are indulgent and excessive. Temperance and economy bring prosperity while indulgence and excess lead to destruction. One must not indulge in excess in these five things. When husband and wife do not indulge in excess, Heaven and earth will be harmonious; when wind and rain are not in excess, the five grains will ripen; and when excessive clothing is not indulged in, the body will be comfortable.

[1] The old Chinese household is a large one. Not counting the relatives and dependents, the household proper consists of the master, the mistress, and a group of concubines and maids whose number increases with the rank and means of the lord.

[2] Namely, in the provision of (1) shelter, (2) clothing, (3) food, (4) boats and vehicles, and (5) in sexual relations.

CHAPTER VII

THREEFOLD ARGUMENT [1]

Ch'eng Fan [2] asked Motse : " Sir, you say the sage-kings did not have music. But, anciently, when the feudal lords were tired of attending to government, they found recreation in music of bells and drums. When the ministers and gentlemen were tired of attending to office they found recreation in music of yü [3] and shê. [4] And the farmers ploughed the fields in spring, weeded them in summer, reaped the harvest in autumn, and stored the grains in winter. Then they would enjoy music of jars and vases. [5] Sir, you say the sage-kings did not have music. This would be comparing them to the horse placed under yoke and never released, and the bow drawn and never unstrung. Is this not impossible for the ordinary human being ? "

Motse replied : In ancient times, Yao and Shun lived in huts and yet they made codes of propriety and composed music. [6] T'ang sent Chieh to exile on the ocean and installed himself ruler of the empire. Having achieved success and without cause for anxiety, he added to the music of the former

---

[1] This chapter merely answers an objection to Motse's " CONDEMNATION OF MUSIC ", chaps. xxxii–iv. It is hardly an appendix. It, if Motse was its author, reminds one of Descartes' publication of the objections to his doctrine and his answers with his main treatise of the *Meditations*.

[2] Ch'eng Fan is a scholar of both Confucianism and Moism.

[3] Yü 竽 is a Chinese hand organ of thirty-six reed pipes.

[4] Shê 瑟 is a Chinese horizontal psaltery of twenty-five strings.

[5] These earthenware were a regular department of ancient Chinese musical instruments.

[6] This does not mean that they did this themselves. It only says that it is done under their auspices.

kings that of his own composition, called " The Salvation ",[1]
and also instituted the " Chiu Chao ". King Wu conquered
the Yin dynasty and executed Chow and installed himself
ruler of the empire.   Having achieved success and having
no cause of anxiety, he added to the music of the former kings
that of his own composition, called " Hsiang ".   King Ch'eng
of Chou again added to the music of the former kings that of
his own compostion, named " Tsou Yü ".   The reign of King
Ch'eng was not so good as that of King Wu, that of King Wu
was not so good as that of T'ang the Successful, and that
of T'ang the Successful was not so good as that of Yao and
Shun.   So, then, he who has the more elaborate music has
the less efficient government.   Judging from this, music
is not anything to govern the empire with.

Ch'eng Fan objected : " Sir, you have said the sage-
kings did not have music. This shows they did. How then
can you say the sage-kings did not have music ? "

Motse said : The desire of the sage-kings [2] was to cut down
excesses.   Eating is of course profitable, but it takes so little
intelligence to eat when one is hungry that it may be said
to be nil.   Now the sage-kings had music, but it was so little
that it may also be said to be nil.

---

[1] This name was given to the composition to commemorate his enterprise
against Chieh the wicked king, the success of which freed the people from
tyranny.

[2] Certain phrases, clauses, or even passages seem to be missing here.

BOOK II

CHAPTER VIII

EXALTATION OF THE VIRTUOUS [1] (I)

Motse said : Now, all the rulers desire their provinces to be wealthy, their people to be numerous, and their jurisdiction to secure order. But what they obtain is not wealth but poverty, not multitude but scarcity, not order but chaos—this is to lose what they desire and obtain what they avert. Why is this ? [2]

Motse said : This is because the rulers have failed to exalt the virtuous and to employ the capable in their government. When the virtuous are numerous in the state, order will be stable ; when the virtuous are scarce, order will be unstable. Therefore the task of the lords lies nowhere but in multiplying the virtuous.

But what is the way to multiply the virtuous ?

Motse said : Supposing it is desired to multiply good archers and good drivers [3] in the country, it will be only

---

[1] The Chinese word hsien 賢 includes more than virtue in its meaning. Wisdom and talent are also implied. It is hard to find an English word for this combination. It is interesting to recall in this connexion the Socratic formula : knowledge is virtue.

[2] In the *Motse* text an interrogation is often used to form the transition between two thoughts, or the main thought and its explanation. It reminds one of the more artistically interpolated remarks by the listeners in Plato's *Dialogues*.

[3] The ancient Chinese education consists of six arts, namely, (1) Propriety, (2) Music, (3) Archery, (4) Driving (a chariot), (5) Composition, and (6) Mathematics. Confucius was himself an able advocate of this curriculum. Compare with Plato's educational programme in his *Republic*.

natural to enrich them, honour them, respect them, and commend them ; then good archers and good drivers can be expected to abound in the country. How much more should this be done in the case of the virtuous and the excellent who are firm in morality, versed in rhetoric, and experienced in statecraft—since these are the treasures of the nation and props of the state ? They should also be enriched, honoured, respected, and commended in order that they may abound.

When the ancient sage-kings [1] administered the government they declared : " The unrighteous will not be enriched, the unrighteous will not be honoured, the unrighteous will not be favoured,[2] the unrighteous will not be placed near." Upon hearing this, the rich and honoured of the country all began to deliberate, saying : " What I have been depending on was wealth and honour. Now the Lord promotes the righteous without discrimination against the poor and humble. Hence I may not do unrighteousness." Upon hearing this, the favoured also began to deliberate, saying : " What I have been depending on was favour. Now the Lord promotes the righteous without discrimination against those thus far

[1] Subsequent text shows Motse here had Yao, Shun, Yü, T'ang, Wen, and Wu in mind. *Infra,* p. 38, note 1.

[2] The Chinese word here is Ch in 親. An ordinary meaning of it is relation, relatives, or to be related. According to this meaning the clause will have to read " relatives if unrighteous will not be recognized as such ". And similarly the sentence after next will have to be rendered " Upon hearing this, the relatives also began to deliberate, saying, ' What I have been depending on was relationship. Now the Lord promotes the righteous without discrimination against those who are unrelated. Hence I may not do unrighteousness.' " But this is clumsy expression in itself and destroys the parallelism of clauses that is a feature of the ethical books in *Motse.* At any rate, the version as given here in the translation seems to include this idea.

neglected. Hence I may not do unrighteousness." Upon
hearing this, those placed near began to deliberate, saying :
" What I have been depending on was intimacy. Now the
Lord promotes the righteous without discrimination against
the distant. Hence I may not do unrighteousness." Upon
hearing this, the distant also began to deliberate, saying :
" I used to think, being distant I had nothing to depend on.
Now the Lord promotes the righteous without discrimination against the distant. Hence I may not do unrighteousness."
Vassals of distant districts as well as youths in the palace,
and multitudes within the state boundaries as well as the
rustics living on the four borders, upon hearing this, all
competed in doing righteousness.

Now what is the reason for all this ?

It is only with material goods that the superior can employ
his subordinates, and it is only with statecraft that the subordinates can serve their lord. Take, for example, the rich
man who built his walls high and left only one gate. When
the burglar had entered, the man closed the gate and searched
for him, and the burglar had no more exit. Why ? Because
the man had the vantage-point.[1]

Therefore in administering the government, the ancient
sage-kings ranked the morally excellent high and exalted the
virtuous. If capable, even a farmer or an artisan would be
employed—commissioned with high rank, remunerated with
liberal emoluments, trusted with important charges, and
empowered to issue final orders. For, if his rank were not

[1] The point of this illustration seems to be that if the ruler made righteousness the only criterion for his favours, he will be sure to secure righteous
people.

high, people would not respect him ; if his emoluments were not liberal, people would not have confidence in him ; if his orders were not final, people would not stand in awe before him. To place these three (honours) upon the virtuous is not so much to reward virtue, as to bring about the success of the enterprise (of government).[1] Therefore ranks should be standardized according to virtue, tasks assigned according to office, and rewards given according to labour spent. When emoluments are distributed in proportion to achievements, officials cannot be in constant honour, and people in eternal humility. If a person is capable promote him, if incapable, lower his rank. Give prominence to public approval and keep back private grudges (in the matter of selecting men). Here, then, is the principle.

So, in days of old, Yao[2] brought forward Shun[2] from Fu Tse[3] and entrusted him with the government, and the world had peace. Yü[2] brought forward Yi[2] from Yin Fang[3] and entrusted him with the government, and the nine districts became organized. T'ang[2] brought forward Yi Yin[2] from the kitchen[4] and entrusted him with the government and his

---

[1] According to Chinese political ideals, the government is looked upon as a mission and trust from Heaven. Its well-being is the highest end of the ruler's conduct which is at once political and ethical.

[2] Names of prominent political and ethical figures in ancient Chinese history.

[3] Names of places the locations of which are now either entirely unknown or subjects of controversy among scholars.

[4] The story is about the very virtuous man whose family name is Yi and whose name is Chih. Yin is the title of the high office that he held under T'ang. And he is popularly known as Yi Yin. According to Lü Pu-Wei, *Ch'un Ch'iu Pen Wei Lu*, 春 秋 本 味 錄, or *Lü Shih Ch'un Ch'iu*, a woman of the tribe of Hsin, found a baby among the mulberry trees while she was gathering the leaves. She offered it to the Prince of the tribe and he

plans were successful. King Wen [1] brought forward Hung Yao [1] and T'ai Tien [1] from their rabbit nets [2] and entrusted them with the government and the Western land [3] showed respect. Therefore, during those days the officials of high rank and liberal emoluments all carefully and anxiously executed their duties; and the farmers and artisans all

reared him. When the baby grew up he was virtuous and this was Yi Yin. T'ang had heard of this virtuous man in the tribe of Hsin and asked to have him but was refused. Later T'ang arranged to marry the daughter of the Prince of Hsin. Yi Yin was sent in the bridal party. Lü's account ends here. But it seems that Yi Yin did not get any immediate notice from T'ang upon arriving at the latter's Court. So he served T'ang in his kitchen and later was discovered by T'ang there.

[1] Names of prominent political and ethical figures in ancient Chinese history.

[2] The seventh ode in *Shih Ching* 詩 經 has for its title " Rabbit Nets ". It consists of three stanzas. According to the translation of James Legge, *The Chinese Classics* (there will be frequent occasions in the following pages to refer to this work. We shall henceforth let " Legge " stand for the complete title. The edition used is that of Hongkong, 1861–5), vol. iv, part i, pp. 13–14, it reads :

" Carefully adjusted are the rabbit nets,
Clang, clang go the blows on the pegs.
That stalwart, martial man
Might be shield and wall to his prince.

Carefully adjusted are the rabbit nets,
And placed where many ways meet.
That stalwart, martial man
Would be good companion for his prince.

Carefully adjusted are the rabbit nets,
And placed in the midst of the forest.
That stalwart, martial man
Might be head and heart to his prince."

It is an exaltation of the justice of King Wen who would exalt persons even from such low ranks as these two rabbit catchers if they are virtuous.

[3] Meaning the neighbours of King Wen who was at the time known as Earl Ch'ang.

encouraged one another in exalting virtue. Therefore, the scholars are really to be officials and governors. As long as there were scholars (in government), the plans (of the ruler) were not defeated and he had no hardships to endure ; his name was established and success achieved ; his excellence became known and yet evils were not spread. This is all due to the employment of the scholars.

Therefore Motse said : The virtuous who are prosperous must be exalted, and the virtuous who are not prosperous must be exalted too. If it is desired to continue the ways of Yao and Shun, to exalt the virtuous is indispensable. Now, exaltation of the virtuous is the root of government.

CHAPTER IX

EXALTATION OF THE VIRTUOUS (II)

Motse said : Now, in caring for the people, ruling the state, and governing the country, the rulers desire permanency and stability. But why do they not learn that exaltation of the virtuous is the foundation of government ?

How do we know exaltation of the virtuous is the foundation of government ?

When the honourable and wise run the government, the ignorant and humble remain orderly ; but when the ignorant and humble run the government, the honourable and wise become rebellious. Therefore we know exaltation of the virtuous is the foundation of government.

The ancient sage-kings greatly emphasized the exaltation of the virtuous and the employment of the capable. Without special consideration for relatives, for the rich and honoured, or for the good-looking, they exalted and promoted the virtuous, enriched and honoured them, and made them governors and leaders. The vicious they kept back and banished, depossessed and degraded, and made labourers and servants. Thereupon people were all encouraged by rewards and threatened by punishments and strove with each other after virtue. Thus the virtuous multiplied and the vicious diminished in number. Such is exaltation of the virtuous. Then the sage-kings watched their words and observed their conduct, found out their capabilities and carefully assigned them their offices. Such is employment of the capable. Accordingly those who were capable to govern the country were made to govern the country, those who were capable to administer the court were made to administer the court, and those who were capable in managing the districts were made to manage the districts. All those who had charge of the country, the court, and the districts were then the virtuous of the land.

When the virtuous rules the country, he starts the day early and retires late, hearing lawsuits and attending to the government. As a result, the country is well governed and laws are justly administered. When the virtuous administers the court he retires late and wakes up early, collecting taxes from passes, markets, and on products from mountains, woods, waters, and land to fill the court. As a result, the court is filled and wealth is not wasted. When the virtuous manages the districts, he goes out before sunrise and comes back after sunset, plowing and sowing, planting and cultivating, and gathering harvests of grains. As a result, grains are in plenty and people are sufficiently supplied with food. Therefore when the country is well governed the laws are well administered, and when the court is filled the people are wealthy. For the higher sphere, the rulers had wherewith to make wine and cakes to do sacrifice and libation to Heaven and the spirits. For the countries outside, they had wherewith to provide the furs and money to befriend neighbouring feudal lords. For the people within, they had wherewith to feed the hungry and give rest to the tired. Above all these, they had means to cherish the virtuous. Therefore from above, Heaven and the spirits enrich them ; from without, the feudal lords submit themselves to them ; from within, the people show them affection, and the virtuous

become loyal to them. Hence they could have satisfaction
in planning and success in execution. In defence they are
strong and in attack victorious. Now the way that enabled
the sage-kings of the Three Dynasties, namely Yao, Shun,
Yü, T'ang, Wen and Wu,[1] to rule the empire and head the
feudal lords was no other than this (principle of exaltation
of the virtuous).

However, if there is only the principle while the technique
of its application is not known, then it would seem to be still
incomplete. Therefore there should be laid down three rules.
What are the three rules ? They are : (1) when their rank
(that of the virtuous) is not high, people would not show
them respect ; (2) when their emoluments are not liberal,
people would not place confidence in them ; (3) when their
orders are not final, people would not stand in awe before
them. So the ancient sage-kings placed them high in rank,
gave them liberal emoluments, trusted them with important
charges, and decreed their orders to be final. And all this
was done not merely to reward their subordinates ; it was to
fulfil their trust.[2]

Thus runs an Ode : " I am instructing you to take worries
and cares of the world as your own ; I am teaching the order
of ranks for the virtuous and talented. Who can handle

---

[1] " The sage-kings of the Three Dynasties " had become a symbol of
virtue even at such an early time as that of Confucius. The kings and
dynasties referred to are Yü of Hsia, T'ang of Shang, and Wen and Wu of
Chou. Yao and Shun are virtuous emperors of an earlier date and do not
belong to the Three Dynasties. Cf. *Motse, the Neglected Rival of Confucius*, chap. i.

[2] *Supra*, p. 33, note 1.

heat without rinsing his hands (in cold water) ? " [1] This is
to show how in the past the rulers could not do without
befriending subordinates and helpers. It was like the necessity
of rinsing in handling hot objects to relieve the hands.

The ancient sage-kings concentrated on acquiring and
employing the virtuous—honouring them with high ranks,
and assigning land to them—unwearied to the end of their
lives. The virtuous men on the other hand only hoped to find
an enlightened ruler to serve—exhausting all the powers of
the four limbs to attend to the king's business—untired to
the end of their lives. When there were any excellences and
virtues they were attributed to the emperor. Thus excellences
and virtues belonged to the emperor while complaints and
slanders were directed against the subordinates. Peace and
joy abode with the king while worries and sorrows were
lodged with the officials. This was how the ancient sage-
kings administered the government. The present rulers,
imitating the ancients, also want to employ the virtuous in
government by exalting them. Ranks given them are very
high, but the emoluments do not follow proportionally. Now,

---

[1] This quotation is evidently from the Ode " Sang Jou " in *Shih Ching*,
though the text in *Shih Ching* shows some modification. According
to Legge, whose translation here does not seem to be quite adequate, the
fifth stanza of " Sang Yew " (vol. iv, part iii, Book iii, ode iii, p. 522)
reads :

" You have your counsels ; you employ caution ;
But the disorder grows and dismemberments ensue.
I tell you the subjects of anxiety ;
I instruct you how to distinguish the orders of men.
Who can hold anything hot ?
Must he not dip it (first) in water ?
How can you (by your method) bring a good state of things about ?
You (and your advisers) will sink together in ruin."

to be high in rank but receive small emoluments will not inspire people's confidence. The virtuous would say to themselves : " This is not real love for me, but only to make use of me as a means." Now, how can people be affectionate to their superiors when they are only (treated as) means ? Therefore an ancient king said : " He who is too ambitious in government will not share his tasks with others. He who over-treasures wealth will not offer big emoluments to others." When tasks are not assigned and emoluments are not given, it may be asked wherefrom would the virtuous come to the side of the rulers ?

And when the virtuous are not at the side of the rulers, the vicious will be on their right and left. When the vicious are on the right and left, then commendations will not fall on the virtuous and punishments will not be upon the wicked. If the rulers follow these in governing the states, in the same way rewards will not go to the virtuous and punishment not to the wicked. When rewards really do not go to the virtuous and punishment not to the wicked, then the virtuous will find no encouragement, neither the wicked any obstruction. At home the vicious are not filial to their parents, and, having left their home town, they would not recognize their elders. They move about without restraint and disregard the rules of propriety about sexes. When trusted with the administration of the court, they would steal ; when trusted to defend a city, they would raise an insurrection. When the lord meets with death, they would not follow him and commit suicide ; when the lord has to flee the country, they would not accompany him in banishment.[1] In judging

---

[1] These are the common law requirements of the Chinese code of loyalty.

lawsuits they are not just, and in dividing property they are partial. In planning they are not helpful, in execution they are inefficient. Neither in defence are they strong, nor in attack are they victorious. Now, the reason that the wicked kings of the Three Dynasties, namely, Chieh, Chow, Yu, and Li,[1] misruled the country and upset their states was no other than this (employment of the vicious).

Why is this so ? Because they understood petty affairs but were ignorant about things of importance. When the rulers cannot get a coat made they will employ able tailors. When they cannot have an ox or a sheep killed they will employ able butchers. In these two instances they do know they should exalt the virtuous and employ the capable for business. But when it comes to the disorder of the country and danger of the state, they do not know they should exalt the virtuous and employ the capable for government. Rather, they would employ their relatives, they would employ the rich without merit, and the good-looking. But as to the employment of the rich without merit and the good-looking— will these necessarily prove themselves wise and intelligent ? To let these rule the country is to let the unwise and unintelligent rule the country. And disorder can then be predicted. Moreover, the rulers employ their minds by the attractiveness of their appearance, and show them favour without finding out their knowledge. As a result, those who are not capable to rule a hundred men are assigned to posts over a thousand, and those who are not capable to rule a thousand are assigned to posts over ten thousand. What is

---

[1] Chieh is of Hsia, Chow of Shang, Yu and Li of Chou.

the reason for this ? Why, such positions are high in rank and rich in emoluments. Therefore the specially favoured are picked for them. But to make those incapable of ruling a thousand men rule ten thousand is to increase their duty tenfold. The business of the government comes daily. It is to be attended to every day, yet the day cannot be lengthened by tenfold. To govern, again, requires knowledge. When knowledge is not increased by ten times, while a tenfold task is assigned, it will evidently result in attending to one and neglecting nine. Though the task be attended to day and night, still it cannot be well executed. And the reason for this is because the rulers do not understand that they should exalt the virtuous and employ the capable in government.

Thus exaltation of the virtuous and employment of the capable with the consequent success in government is presented above in the earlier paragraphs. And the depreciation of the virtuous with the resulting confusion in government is presented here in these paragraphs. If the rulers now want to govern their states so that they will be permanent and unshakeable, why do they not learn that exaltation of the virtuous is the foundation of government ?

Besides, is this principle merely a conception of Motse ? It is the way of the sage-kings and the tenet of " Chü Nien ",[1] a book of an ancient king. And, thus it is recorded : " (He) sought out the wise men to protect and aid you." [2] And thus

---

[1] Further, on p. 52 " Shu Nien " and p. 65 " Hsiang Nien " are also mentioned. They all seem to refer to an Essay in *Shu Ching* 書 經. But the Essay is not found in the present text of *Shu Ching*.

[2] This quotation is from " The Instructions of Yi " in *Shu Ching*. For the full context see Legge, vol. iii, part i, p. 196.

states the " Oath of T'ang " : " I then sought for the Great
Sage, with whom I might unite my strength and mind to
govern the empire." [1] All these show how the sage-kings
never failed to exalt the virtuous and employ the capable
in government. The sage-kings of old comprehended only
this—to exalt the virtuous and employ the capable in government and nobody else ; so the whole world was benefited.

In times of old, Shun cultivated land at Mt. Li,[2] made
pottery by the River, [2] and was engaged in fishing in Lake
Lei.[2] Yao discovered him at Fu Tse.[2] Exalting him, Yao made
him Emperor and handed to him the government of the
empire and the rule over the people. Yi Chih once served in
the bridal party of the daughter of the Prince of Hsin,[3] and later
voluntarily served T'ang as his cook. T'ang discovered him.
Exalting him, T'ang made him his Prime Minister and handed
to him the government of the empire and the rule over the
people. Fu Yüeh once wore garments of coarse cloth tied
with ropes, working as an artisan at Fu Yen.[2] Wu Ting discovered him.[4] Exalting him, Wu Ting made him High Duke

[1] This quotation is not found in the " Oath of T'ang " but with some
modifications in the " Proclamation of T'ang" in the present text of *Shu
Ching*. See Legge, vol. iii, part i, p. 187.

[2] Names of places the location of which are now either entirely unknown
or subject to controversy among scholars. *Supra*, p. 33, note 3.

[3] *Supra*, p. 33, note 4.

[4] This story is about the virtuous man, Fu Yüeh. Yüeh is the name of
the man and Fu is the surname given him by Emperor Wu Ting because
he was discovered at Fu Yen—a common practice in those ancient days.
According to Huang Fu Mi, the Emperor had a dream of a virtuous man
sent to him by Heaven in a prisoner's apparel. And the man told him,
" I am a prisoner by the name of Fu Yüeh ". When the dream was told
to the ministers, none thought it could be real. But the Emperor ordered
to have the man's likeness painted to search for him all over the empire.
Finally a prisoner-labourer was found at Fu Yen by the name of Yüeh.

and handed to him the government of the empire and the
rule over the people.

Why is it that these people starting in humility arrived at
honour, starting in poverty arrived at wealth ? It is because
these rulers understood the importance of exalting the
virtuous and employing the capable in government. Therefore,
none of the people were hungry yet without food, cold yet
without clothing, tired yet without rest, disturbed yet without
peace. And, the ancient sage-kings in exalting the virtuous
and employing the capable in government were following
the ways of Heaven. Even Heaven does not discriminate
among the poor and the rich, the honourable and
the humble, the distant and the near, and the related
and the unrelated (to those in power). The virtuous
were promoted and exalted ; the vicious were kept back
and banished.

Now, who were those that, possessing wealth and position,
still strove after virtues and were rewarded ? They were the
sage-kings of the Three Dynasties, namely, Yao, Shun, Yü,
T'ang, Wen and Wu.[1] How were they rewarded ? When
they governed the empire, they loved all the people universally
and benefited them, and led them in doing honour to Heaven
and service to the spirits. As they loved and benefited the
people, Heaven and the spirits rewarded them, appointing
them to be Sons of Heaven, and parents of the-people. And,
thereupon people praised them, calling them sage-kings even
unto this day. These then were those that, possessing wealth
and position, still strove after virtues and were rewarded.
Now, who were those that, possessing wealth and position,

[1] *Supra*, p. 38, note 1.

yet practised evil and were punished ? They were the wicked kings of the Three Dynasties,[1] namely, Chieh, Chow, Yu, and Li. How do we know they were those ? When they governed the empire they disliked all the people inclusively and oppressed them and led them to curse Heaven and the spirits. Oppressing and destroying the people, they were punished by Heaven and the spirits; their corpses were mangled and lacerated, their children and grand-children were scattered and dispersed, their family hearths were extinguished and descendants exterminated. And, thereupon the people railed at them, calling them wicked kings even unto this day. These, then, are those that, possessing wealth and position, yet practised evil and were punished.

Now, who were those that were related (to the ruler) but not virtuous and were visited by punishment ? Count Kun [2] was of direct royal descent but had degenerated in the royal virtues. So he was banished to the wilderness of Yü Yü where (in the prison) light could not reach him, neither did the emperor show any favour. Such was he who was related but not virtuous and was visited by punishment. Now, who were those that were employed by Heaven because of their capability ? Yü, Chi, and Kao T'ao were they. How do we know that ? It is found in the " Penal Code of Lü ", a book of an early king, thus : " The Emperor (Yao) inquired among his subjects, and complaints were made against the Miaos (barbarians)." Again, " As the feudal lords have been appointed without insight, even the widows and the widowers are not protected. Dignity is revered only when it is

---

[1] *Supra*, p. 41, note 1.
[2] Kun is the father of the virtuous Emperor and Great Engineer Yü.

accompanied with magnanimity; enlightenment is respected only when it is accompanied with magnanimity. Thereupon three chiefs were commissioned to care for and consolate the people : (1) Po Yi delivered the laws and statutes and taught therewith the people ; (2) Yü reduced the Flood and recovered the land, and gave names to hills and rivers ; (3) Chi descended (from his rank) and sowed seeds to encourage good farming. The benefits of the achievements of these three chiefs all fell upon the people." [1] This is to say that the three sages were careful in speech, vigilant in conduct, penetrating in thought, studying and planning for every detail and benefit of the world—with this to do service to Heaven on high, Heaven will bless their virtue ; to bestow it to the people below, the people will be visited by its benefits lasting beyond their lifetime.

[1] The " Penal Code of Lü " is an Essay in *Shu Ching*. Legge's translation shows considerable divergence from the rendition given here. The quotation seems to be lengthy and important enough to be given a different version for comparison. The following is taken from Legge, vol. iii, pp. 593-7 :—

" From the princes down to the inferior officers, all helped with clear intelligence the spread of the regular principles of duty, and the solitary and the widows were no more disregarded. The great emperor with an unprejudiced mind carried his inquiries low down among the people, and the solitary and widows laid before him their complaints against the Meaos. He sought to awe (the people) by his virtue, and all were filled with dread, he proceeded (also) to enlighten them by his virtue, and all were enlightened. And he charged the three chiefs to labour with compassionate anxiety in the people's behalf. The Baron E delivered the statutes (of ceremony) to prevent the people from rendering themselves obnoxious to punishment. Yu reduced to order the water and the land, distinguishing by name the hills and rivers. Tseih spread abroad a knowledge of husbandry, so that the people could largely cultivate the admirable grains. When the three chiefs had accomplished their work, it was abundantly well with the people."

Thus said the ancient kings : " Now, this way, when followed broadly to govern the world, will not be found to be too slender ; when followed narrowly, will not be too unwieldly ; when followed with discretion, will benefit the people beyond their lifetime." Referring to it, the " Eulogy of Chou " sings : " The virtue of the sage shining upon the world is lofty as Heaven, wide as earth, high as the mountain, unbreakable and infallible ; luminating as the sun, brilliant as the moon, eternal with heaven and earth." This is to describe how enlightening and all-embracing, deep-rooted and, therefore, permanent is the virtue of the sage. Therefore the virtue of the sage is really inclusive of heaven and earth.

Now, the rulers want to be lord over the empire and be head of the feudal lords. But how can it be done without virtue and righteousness ? Their way must be by over-powering and overawing. But what makes them adopt this ? It simply pursues the people to death. But life is what the people eagerly desire, and death what they greatly dread. What is desired is not obtained, but what is dreaded befalls them ever so often. From antiquity to the present, none has yet been able to be lord over the empire and head of the feudal lords by this way. Now the rulers desire to be lord of the world and head of the feudal lords and want to have their ideas prevail all over the world, and their names established in posterity. But why do they not learn that exaltation of the virtuous is the foundation of government ? This was the actual conduct of the sages.

CHAPTER X

EXALTATION OF THE VIRTUOUS (III)

Motse said : All the rulers in the world desire their states to be wealthy, their people to be many, and their government and jurisdiction to be orderly. But they do not understand to govern their states and people by exaltation of the virtuous. They have missed, indeed, the foundation of government. But can we not point this out to them by means of parallels ? Now, supposing, in governing his state, a feudal lord should proclaim : "All those who can shoot (with an arrow) and drive (a chariot) well I shall reward and honour ; all those who can not I shall punish and disgrace." If, then, we should inquire among the people of the state as to who would rejoice and who would be afraid, I suppose naturally those who could shoot and drive would rejoice and those who could not would be afraid. I have followed this (line of argument) and led them supposedly to proclaim : " All the loyal and faithful I shall reward and honour ; all the disloyal and unfaithful I shall punish and disgrace." If now we should inquire among the people of the state as to who would rejoice and who would be afraid, I suppose naturally the loyal and faithful would rejoice and the disloyal and unfaithful would be afraid. Therefore the state and the people are to be governed by exalting the virtuous, so that those in the state that do good will be encouraged and those that do evil will be obstructed.

To govern the empire seems then to consist of encouraging the good and obstructing the evil. But why is it that I have esteemed the way of Yao, Shun, Yü, T'ang, Wen, and Wu ? [1]

[1] *Supra*, p. 38, note 1.

Because they administered the government in such a way that those in the empire that did good would be encouraged and those that did evil would be obstructed. So, then, the principle of exaltation of the virtuous is identical with the way of Yao, Shun, Yü, T'ang, Wen, and Wu.

The gentlemen [1] of to-day all exalt the virtuous in their private speech and conduct. But when it comes to the administration of the government for the public, they fail to exalt the virtuous and employ the capable. Then I know the gentlemen understand only trifles and not things of significance.

How do I know it is so ?

Suppose the ruler had a cow or a sheep which he could not have killed, he would surely look for a skilful butcher. Or if he wanted a garment which he could not have made, he would surely look for a skilful tailor. For these, the ruler would not employ his relatives, the rich without merit, and the good-looking, because he knew clearly they were incapable. He was afraid they would spoil the things to be attended to. So, in these, the rulers do not fail to exalt the virtuous and employ the capable. Again, if the ruler had a sick horse that he could not have cured, he would surely look for an experienced veterinary doctor. Or if he had a tight bow which he could not draw, he would surely look for a skilful workman. For these, the ruler would not employ his relatives, the rich without merit, and the good-looking, because he knew clearly they were incapable. He was afraid they would spoil the things

---

[1] Meaning the learned people who are the officials and advisers to the rulers.

to be attended to. So, in these matters the rulers do not fail
to exalt the virtuous and employ the capable. But when it
comes to the affairs of the state all is different. The relations
of the rulers, the rich without merit, and the good-looking
are all promoted. Then does it not seem that the rulers love
their states not even as much as they love a tight bow, a sick
horse, a garment, or a cow or a sheep ? Therefore I know the
gentlemen of the world understand only trifles and not things
of significance. This is like trying to make messengers of the
dumb and musical directors of the deaf.

To the contrary, in governing the empire the sage-kings
of old enriched and honoured those who were not necessarily
their relatives, the rich without merit, or the good-looking.
At one time Shun cultivated land at Mt. Li,[1] made pottery by
the River, engaged in fishing in Lake Lei,[1] and went peddling
in Ch'ang Yang.[1] Yao discovered him at Fu Tse,[1] made him
emperor, and handed him the government of the empire and
the rule over the people. Yi Yin [2] once took part in the bridal
party of the daughter of the Prince of Hsin, and then was
employed as a cook. T'ang discovered him and exalted him to
be High Duke, handing him the government of the empire
and the rule over the people. Once Fu Yüeh [3] lived in the
District of Pê Hai [1] and built the prison walls. His clothing
was of coarse cloth and tied with ropes. Wu Ting discovered
him and exalted him to be High Duke, handing him the

---

[1] Ancient names of places the location of which is now quite uncertain.
Supra, p. 33, note 3 ; p. 43, note 2.

[2] For story see p. 33, note 4.

[3] For story see p. 43, note 4.

government of the empire and the rule over the people. Now, when Yao exalted Shun, T'ang exalted Yi Yin, and Wu Ting exalted Fu Yüeh was it because they were their relatives, the rich without merit, or the good-looking ? It was only because that by adopting their views, carrying out their plans, and following their ways, Heaven on high would be blessed, the spirits in the middle would be blessed, and the people below would be blessed. Therefore they were promoted and exalted.

Having understood the principle of exalting the virtuous in government, the ancient sage-kings inscribed it on bamboos and silk [1] and engraved it on the dishes and vases,[2] to hand it down to their descendants. Thus we find in the " Penal Code of Lü ",[3] a book of an ancient king,[4] the following : " The King said : ' Ho ! come, ye rulers of states and territories, I will tell you how to make punishments a blessing. Now it is yours to give repose to the people :—what should you be most concerned about the choosing of ? Should it not be proper men ? What should you deal with the most reverently ? Should it not be punishments ? What should you calculate the most ? Should it not be to whom they should reach ? ' " [5] (This is to say) with insight in choosing men and considerateness in meting punishments, you can catch up with the ways

---

[1] These were the only material for writing in those ancient days in China.

[2] Mottoes and maxims were often cut into metal or stone vessels usually for self-remindment.

[3] *Supra*, p. 46, note 1.

[4] This refers to King Mu of Chou in whose reign the Code was made, 951 B.C.

[5] The translation of this passage is entirely taken from Legge, vol. iii, p. 601.

of Yao, Shun, Yü, T'ang, Wen, and Wu. How ? By exaltation of the virtuous. Again in the book " Shu Nien ",[1] another
book of an ancient king, we find : " He looked for wise men
to protect and aid you." [2] This is to say, when the ancient
kings reigned over the empire they invariably selected the
virtuous and made them officials and aids.

The gentlemen in the world like riches and honour, and
dislike poverty and humility. Now how can you obtain the
former and avoid the latter ? There is no better way than to
practise virtue. What then is the way to practise virtue ?
Let him who has strength be alert to help others, let him who
has wealth endeavour to share it with others, let him who
possesses the Tao (the way of nature and life) teach others
persuasively. With this, the hungry will be fed, the cold
will be clothed, the disturbed will have order. When the
hungry are fed, the cold are clothed, and the disturbed
have order—this is procuring abundant life. But those
whom the rulers now are enriching and honouring are
all their relatives, the rich without merit, and the good-
looking. What can there be that guarantees these to be
wise ? When the unwise are charged with the government
of the country, disorder in the country can be predicted.
Now the gentlemen of the world like riches and honour,
and dislike poverty and humility. But how can you obtain
the former and avoid the latter ? There seems to be no

---

[1] " Shu Nien " might be originally an essay in *Shu Ching*. But it is not
in the text that we now have. *Supra*, p. 42, note 1.

[2] A sentence quite like this is now found in the " Instructions of Yi "
in *Shu Ching*. Cf. Legge, vol. iii, p. 196.

other way than to be the rulers' relatives, the rich without
merit, and the good-looking. Evidently one cannot become
these by learning.

So, when the art of judging is not understood, although
some virtuous people may even compare with Yü, T'ang,
Wen, and Wu, there will be no commendation. And, although
a relative of the ruler may be lame and dumb, deaf and blind,
and evil like Chieh and Chow, there will be no condemnation.
Therefore reward does not fall on the virtuous or punishment
on the evil. As those rewarded are without merit, those
punished are naturally without guilt. And so, people all
became disintegrated in heart and ·dissipated in body, and
despairing in doing good. With all their strength unused, they
would not help one another ; with all unused supplies rotting
and fermenting, they would not share with one another ;
hiding the excellent Tao they would not show it to others.
As a result of this, the hungry are not fed, the cold are not
clothed, and the disturbed are not given order.

In the days of old, Yao had Shun, Shun had Yü, Yü had
Kao T'ao, T'ang had Yi Yin, King Wu had Hung Yao, T'ai
Tien, Nan Kung K'uo and San Yi Sheng—therefore the world
was harmonious and people were prosperous. And those near
felt contented and those distant were attracted. Wherever
the sun and the moon shone, boats and vehicles could reach,
rain and dew visited, and life depended on grains [1]; few
were not converted (to good) by this. Hence if the rulers in
the world now desire to do magnanimity and righteousness

---

[1] This marks off the civilized world from the barbarians. The modern
phraseology for this would be, " where civilization has attained the
agricultural stage ".

and be superior men, and desire to strike the way of the sage-kings on the one hand and work for the benefit of the country and the people on the other ; then it is indispensable that the principle of Exaltation of the Virtuous be understood. Now, exaltation of the virtuous is indeed the blessing of Heaven, the spirits, and the people, as well as the foundation of government.

BOOK III

CHAPTER XI

IDENTIFICATION WITH THE SUPERIOR [1] (I)

Motse said : In the beginning of human life, when there was yet no law and government, the custom was " everybody according to his own idea " [2]. Accordingly each man had his own idea, two men had two different ideas and ten men had ten different ideas—the more people the more different notions. And everybody approved of his own view and disapproved the views of others, and so arose mutual disapproval among men. As a result, father and son and elder and younger brothers became enemies and were estranged from each other, since they were unable to reach any agreement. Everybody worked for the disadvantage of the others with water, fire, and poison. Surplus energy was not spent for mutual aid ; surplus goods were allowed to rot without sharing ; excellent teachings (Tao) were kept secret and not revealed. The disorder in the (human) world could be

[1] In Chinese the title of these three essays is literally Superior Identification 尚 同 . Commentators agree in interpreting it as Identification with the Superior. The contents, however, seem to show the process to be both ways. Motse advocates an identification of the ruler with the will of the poeple as much as one of the people with that of Heaven. The real consistency is based on the assumption that the will of Heaven is embodied in human nature, in the will of the unspoiled common man. " Solidarity " is sometimes used for this title. But this is due to a misreading of the word shang 尚 which here stands really for shang 上. Therefore, 尚 同 is not parallel with 尚 賢, title of the last three chapters, and is not translatable into " Exaltation of Unity " or " Solidarity ".

[2] The Chinese word here is yi 義. It occurs many times in the next three chapters. Considerable difficulty is experienced in making a coherent translation of it. Finally the effort is given up, and it is rendered differently as " notion ", " idea ", " view ", " purpose ", and " standard ", in different connexions.

compared to that among birds and beasts. Yet all this disorder was due to the want of a ruler.

Therefore (Heaven) [1] chose the virtuous in the world and crowned him emperor. Feeling the insufficiency of his capacity, the emperor chose the virtuous in the world and installed them as the three ministers. Seeing the vastness of the empire and the difficulty of attending to matters of right and wrong and profit and harm among peoples of far countries, the three ministers divided the empire into feudal states and assigned them to feudal lords. Feeling the insufficiency of their capacity, the feudal lords, in turn, chose the virtuous of their states and appointed them as their officials. When the rulers were all installed, the emperor issued a mandate to all the people, saying : " Upon hearing good or evil one shall report it to a superior. What the superior thinks to be right all shall think to be right ; what the superior thinks to be wrong all shall think to be wrong. When the superior is at fault there shall be good counsel, when the subordinates show virtue there shall be popular recommendation. To identify one's self with the superior and not to unite one's self with the subordinates—this is what deserves encouragement from above and praise from below. On the other hand, if upon hearing good or evil one should not report to a superior ; if what the superior thought to be right one should not think to be right ; if what the superior thought to be wrong one

[1] This insertion and that on page 59 are mine. In the text there is no subject to the sentence—a peculiar feature of Chinese grammar. I make this insertion on the authority of a parallel passage in the last of these three synoptic chapters of the text, p. 71. This point is dwelt on in view of the fact that some writers incline to interpret Motse's origin of government as a democratic election. Cf. *Motse, the Neglected Rival of Confucius*, chap. vi.

should not think to be wrong ; if when the superior was at
fault there should be no good counsel ; if when the subordinates
showed virtue there should be no popular recommendation ;
if there should be common cause with subordinates and no
identification with the superior—this is what deserves punishment from above and condemnation from below." The
superior made this the basis of reward and punishment. He
was clear-sighted and won his people's confidence.

Now the head of the village was the most high-minded
and tender-hearted man of the village. He notified the people
of the village, saying : " Upon hearing good or evil you shall
report it to the head of the district. What the head of the
district thinks to be right, all shall think to be right. What
he thinks to be wrong, all shall think to be wrong. Put away
from your speech that which is not good and learn his good
speech. Remove from your conduct that which is not good
and learn his good conduct. How then can there be disorder
in the district ? "

Now, how was order brought about in the district ? There
was order in the district because the head could unify the
standards of the district. The head of the district was the
most high-minded and tender-hearted man of the district.
He notified the people of the district, saying : " Upon
hearing good or evil you shall report it to the lord. What the
lord thinks to be right all shall think to be right ; what he
thinks to be wrong all shall think to be wrong. Remove from
your speech that which is not good and learn his good speech.
Take away from your conduct that which is not good and
learn his good conduct. How then can there be disorder in
the state ? "

Now, how was order brought about in the feudal state ? There was order in the state because the feudal lord could unify the standards in the state. The lord of the state was the most high-minded and tender-hearted man of the state. He notified the people of the state, saying : " Upon hearing good or evil you shall report it to the emperor. What the emperor thinks to be right all shall think to be right ; what the emperor thinks to be wrong all shall think to be wrong. Take away from your speech that which is not good and learn his good speech. Remove from your conduct that which is not good and learn his good conduct. How then can there be disorder in the empire ? "

Now, how is order brought about in the empire ? There was order in the empire because the emperor could unify the standards in the empire. If, however, the people all identify themselves with the Son of Heaven but not with Heaven itself, then the jungle [1] is still unremoved. Now, the frequent visitations of hurricanes and torrents are just the punishments from Heaven upon the people for their not identifying their standards with the Will of Heaven. Therefore, Motse said : The sage-kings of old devised the five punishments [2] to rule the people in order to be able to lay hands on those who did not identify themselves with their superiors—a device of the same nature as threads are tied into skeins and a net is controlled by a main rope.

[1] Jungle is here used figuratively for disorder in contrast to cultivated land as order.

[2] The five punishments differ with different dynasties. But ordinarily they refer to (1) tattooing on the face, (2) cutting off the nose, (3) cutting off the feet, (4) castration, and (5) death. Most of them have long fallen into disuse.

CHAPTER XII

IDENTIFICATION WITH THE SUPERIOR (II)

Motse said : As we look back to the time when there was yet no ruler, it seems the custom was " everybody in the world according to his own standard ". Accordingly each man had his own standard, ten men had ten different standards, a hundred men had a hundred different standards—the more people the more standards. And everybody approved of his own view and disapproved those of others, and so arose mutual disapproval. Even father and son and brothers became enemies, since they were unable to reach any agreement. Surplus energy was not employed for mutual help ; excellent teachings (Tao) were kept secret ; surplus goods were allowed to rot without sharing. The disorder in the (human) world could be compared with that among birds and beasts. The lack of regulations governing the relationships between ruler and subject, between superior and subordinate, and between elder and younger ; and the absence of rules governing the relationships between father and son and between older and younger brothers, resulted in disorder in the world.

Knowing the cause of the confusion to be in the absence of a ruler who could unify the standards in the world, (Heaven) [1] chose the virtuous, sagacious, and wise in the world and crowned him emperor, charging him with the duty of unifying the wills in the empire. Having been crowned, the emperor, realizing the impossibility of unifying the world just by his own senses of hearing and sight, chose the understanding,

[1] *Supra*, p. 56, note 1.

virtuous, sagacious, and wise of the world and installed them as the three ministers, sharing with them the duty of unifying the standards in the empire. The emperor and the three ministers being in office, they felt the vastness of the empire and the difficulty of unifying all the peoples in mountains and woods and those far distant. Therefore they systematically divided up the empire, and appointed numerous feudal lords, charging these with the duty of unifying the standards in each state. The feudal lords in turn felt the difficulty of unifying the standards in their states just by their own senses of hearing and sight. Therefore they chose the virtuous of the state to be their ministers and secretaries and all the way down to the heads of districts and villages, sharing with them the duty of unifying the standards in the state.

When the lords of the country and the heads of the people had been appointed, the emperor issued mandates, instructing the people : " Discovering good you must report it to your superior, discovering evil you must report it to your superior. What the superior thinks to be right all shall think to be right ; what the superior thinks to be wrong all shall think to be wrong. When there is virtue among the people there shall be popular recommendation ; when the superior is at fault there shall be good counsel. You shall identify yourself with the superior and not associate with your subordinates. So doing, one deserves encouragement from his superiors and praise from the people. On the other hand, if upon discovering good you should not report it and upon discovering evil you should not report it ; if you should not think to be right what the superior thinks to be right, and wrong what the superior thinks to be wrong ; if there should be no recommendation when there is virtue among the people and no good counsel when the superior is at fault ; and if you should unite with the subordinates but differ from the superior—you deserve heavy punishment from your superiors and condemnation from the people." Therefore the sage-kings of old were very judicious and faithful in their punishments and rewards. And so all the people aspired to the rewards and commendation from the superior and dreaded his condemnation and punishment.

Thereupon, in accord with the policy of the emperor, the village head proceeded to unify the purposes in the village. Having accomplished this, he led the people of the village to identify themselves with the head of the district, saying : " All you people of the village are to identify yourselves with the head of the district, and are not to unite with the subordinates. What the head of the district thinks to be right all shall think to be right ; what he thinks to be wrong all shall think to be wrong. Put away your evil speech and learn his good speech ; put away your evil conduct and learn his good conduct. For the head of the district is naturally the (most) virtuous of the district. If all the people in the district follow the example of their head, how then can the district be disorderly ? "

Now, how is it that the head of the district was so successful in governing the district ? It was just because he could unify the purposes of the whole district that the district was so orderly. Having accomplished this he in turn led the people of his district to identify themselves with the feudal lord, saying : " All you people of the district shall identify yourselves with the lord of the state, and shall not unite with the subordinates. What the lord thinks to be right all shall think to be right ; what he thinks to be wrong all shall think to be wrong. Put away your evil speech and learn his good speech ; put away your evil conduct and learn his good conduct. For the lord of the state is naturally the (most) virtuous of the state. If all the people in the state follow the example of their lord, how then can the state be in disorder ? "

Now, why was the feudal lord so successful in governing the state ? It was just because he could unify the purposes in the state that the state is orderly. Having accomplished this he in turn led the people of his state to identify themselves with the emperor, saying : " All you people of the state shall identify yourselves with the emperor and shall not unite with the subordinates. What the emperor thinks to be right all shall think to be right ; what he thinks to be wrong all shall think to be wrong. Put away your evil speech and learn his good speech ; put away your evil conduct and learn his good conduct. For the emperor is naturally the (most) high-minded and tender-hearted man of the empire. If all the people of the empire follow his example, how then can the state be disorderly ? "

Now, why was the emperor so successful in governing the empire ? It was just because he could unify the purposes in the empire that the empire is orderly.

But to carry the process of identification with the superior up to the Son of Heaven and not further up to Heaven itself— then the jungle [1] from Heaven is yet unremoved. Thereupon Heaven would send down cold and heat without moderation,

---

[1] Figure for disorder. *Supra*, p. 58, note 1.

and snow, frost, rain, and dew untimely. As a result, the five grains [1] could not ripen and the six animals [2] could not mature; and there would be disease, epidemics, and pestilence. Now the repeated visitations of hurricanes and torrents are just punishments from Heaven—punishments to the people below for not identifying themselves with it. Therefore the sage-kings of old appreciated what Heaven and the spirits desire and avoided what they abominate, in order to increase benefits and to avoid calamities in the world. With purification and baths [3] and clean wine and cakes they led the people to make sacrifice and libation to Heaven and the spirits. In such services to the spirits they dared not use wine and cakes that were unclean, sacrificial animals that were not fat, or jade and silk that did not satisfy the standard requirements. The proper time for the spring and autumn sacrifices they dared not miss. Judging lawsuits, they dared not be unjust. Distributing properties, they dared not be unfair. Even when at leisure they dared not be disrespectful. When the sage-kings made such (good) rulers, Heaven and the spirits commended their leadership from above, and the people cherished it from below. To work under the hearty approval of the Heaven and the spirits is

[1] *Supra*, p. 18, note 1.

[2] The "six animals" refer to (1) horse, (2) ox, (3) sheep, (4) chicken, (5) dog, and (6) pig.

[3] This purification is a preparation to make the person fit to do the sacrifice. It lasts sometimes three days, and sometimes even seven days. Clean clothes are put on after bathing. Wine and meat are not taken. It is expected to work up an intense concentration of attention to enable the worshipper to come into contact with the spirits. For a more detailed discussion on this point cf. Y. P. Mei: " Ancestor Worship—Origin and Value," *Chinese Students' Monthly*, vol. xxi, No. 6, April, 1926, p. 23.

to obtain their blessings. To work under the appreciation of
the people is to obtain their confidence. Administering the
government like this, consequently they would succeed in
planning, accomplish their ends in executing, be strong in
defence and victorious in attack. And the reason for all this
lies in their employing the principle of Identification with the
Superior in government. And this is how the sage-kings of
old administered their government.

People might then ask: At the present time rulers are
not absent from the empire, why then is there disorder in
the empire? Motse said: The political leaders of the present
day are quite different from those of old.[1] The case is parallel
to that of the Five Punishments [2] with the Prince of Miao.[3]
In ancient times, the sage-kings made the code of the Five
Punishments and put the empire in order. But when the
Prince of Miao established the Five Punishments they
unsettled his empire. Can it be that the Punishments are
at fault? Really the fault lies in their application. The
"Penal Code of Lü" among the books of the ancient kings,
says: "Among the people of Miao punishments were applied
without employing instruction and admonition. They made
a code of five tortures and called it law." [4] This is to say,
those who know how to apply punishments can govern the
people with them. And those who do not know, make five
tortures out of them. Can it be that the punishments are at
fault? Only, when their application is not to the point do

---

[1] This is a very explicit reflection on the political conditions of the time.
[2] *Supra*, p. 58, note 2.
[3] The name of an aboriginal tribe.
[4] Compare with Legge, vol. iii, p. 591.

they become five tortures. And, also, " Shu Ling," [1] among
the books of the ancient kings, says : " The same mouth can
produce friendship or produce war." This is to say that he
who can use the mouth well will produce friendship, and he
who cannot will stir up the enemies and the besieging
barbarians. Can it be that the mouth is at fault ? The fault
really lies in its use which stirs up the enemies and the besieging
barbarians.

Hence the installing of the ruler in the ancient days was
intended to govern [2] the people. Just as there is one thread
to hold together the others in a skein and a main rope to a
fishing net, so the ruler is to hold together all the evil and
wicked in the empire and bring their purposes into harmony
(with their superiors). Thus "Hsiang Nien",[3] among the books
of the ancient kings, says : " Now the empire is established
and the capital is located : (Heaven) installed the emperor,
kings, and lords not in order to make them proud, and (Heaven)
appointed the ministers and the officials not in order to make
them idle—it was to apportion duties among them and charge
them with the maintenance of the Heavenly justice." This
is to say that when God and the spirits in the past established
the capital and installed the rulers, it was not to make their
ranks high, and their emoluments substantial, and to give
them wealth and honour, and let them live in comfort and

---

[1] Such a title does not exist among the Essays of the text of *Shu Ching*.
This sentence is now found in the essay "Counsels of Great Yü", Legge,
vol. iii, p. 63. But Sun Yi-Jang points out with insight that the quotation originally belongs to the "Charge to Yü", Legge, vol. iii, p. 256.

[2] The Chinese word chih 治 means to govern and also to govern well,
to take good care of the people.

[3] *Supra*, p. 42, note 1.

free of care. It was really to procure benefits and eliminate
adversities for the people, and to enrich the poor and increase
the few, and to bring safety where there is danger and to
restore order where there is confusion—it was for this that
the political leaders were appointed. And so the ancient
sage-kings administered their government accordingly.

The lords at the present, however, do just the reverse.
Administration is carried on to court flattery. Fathers and
brothers and other relatives and friends are placed at the
right and left and appointed rulers of the people. Knowing
that the superior appointed the rulers not for the welfare
of the people, the people all kept aloof and would not identify
themselves with the superior. Therefore purposes of the
superior and the subordinates are not unified. This being
so, rewards and commendations would not encourage the
people to do good, and punishments and fines would not
restrain them from doing evil.

How do we know this would be so ?

In governing the country, the ruler proclaims : " Whoever
deserves reward I will reward." Suppose the purposes of the
superior and the subordinates are different,whoever is rewarded
by the superior would be condemned by the public. And in
community life the condemnation of the public is supreme.
Though there is reward from the superior, it will not be an
encouragement. In governing the country, again, the ruler
proclaims : " Whoever deserves punishment I will punish."
Suppose the purposes of the superior and the subordinates
are different, whoever is punished by the superior would be
applauded by the public. And in community life the approval
of the public is supreme. Though there is punishment from

the superior, it will not be an obstruction. Now, in governing the country and ruling the people, if rewards cannot encourage the people to do good and punishments cannot restrain them from doing evil, is this not just the same as in the beginning of human life when there were no rulers ?   If it is the same with rulers or without them, it is not the way to govern the people and unify the multitude.

As the ancient sage-kings could observe the principle of Identification with the Superior, when they became rulers the purposes of the superior and the subordinates became interchangeable. If the superior reserved for himself special facilities the subordinates could share them. If the people had any unrighted wrongs or accumulated injuries, the superior would remove them. Therefore, if there was a virtuous man thousands of li away, though his clansmen did not all know it (the fact) and people in the same district did not all know it, the emperor could reward him. And if there was an evil man thousands of li away, though his clansmen did not all know it (the fact) and people in the same village did not all know it, the emperor could punish him. Thereupon all the people in the world were astonished, and carefully avoided doing evil, saying : " The emperor is like a spirit in his hearing and sight." But the ancient kings said : " It was no spirit but only the ability to make use of others' ears and eyes to help one's own hearing and sight, to make use of others' lips to help one's own speech, to make use of others' minds to help one's own thought, to make use of others' limbs to help one's own actions." When there are many to help one's hearing and sight then of course one can hear and see far ; when there are many to help one's speech then one's

good counsel can comfort many ; when there are many to help
one's thought then one's plans can be shaped speedily ; when
there are many to help one's actions then one can accomplish
one's undertaking quickly. So there was no other reason for
the success and great fame of the ancient sages than that they
could carry out the principle of Identification with the Superior
in their administration.

One of the " Eulogies of Chou " among the works of the
ancient kings says : " They came to see His Majesty. Daily
they sought the code of propriety." [1] This describes how in
times of old, the feudal lords came to the emperor's court
both spring and autumn to receive strict instructions from
the emperor and ruled their states accordingly when they
returned ; and there was none among those who came under
such an administration that dared not submit completely.
And, at that time, none dared to confuse the instructions
from the emperor. And thus runs an Ode : " My team
is of white horses with black manes. The six reins
look luxuriant. They trot and gallop. The considerations
(of the emperor) are all-inclusive." [1] Further : " My team is
of dark grey horses. The six reins look like silk. They trot
and gallop. The plans (of the emperor) are all-inclusive." [2]

---

[1] These are the first two lines of the Ode called " Tsai Chien " in
Shih Ching. It narrates the incident of a sacrifice by King Ch'eng in the
royal ancestral temple. The first two lines describe the loyalty shown by
the feudal lords to their emperor on such an occasion. According to Legge,
vol. iv, p. 591, the two lines read :

" They appeared before their Sovereign King,
To seek from him the rules (they were to observe)."

[2] These are the third and fourth stanzas in the reversed order of the
ode called " Huang Huang Che Hua " in *Shih Ching*. It describes and

This is to say that upon discovering either good or evil the ancient feudal lords always hurriedly drove to the emperor and reported it to him. Therefore rewards fell upon the virtuous and punishment upon the wicked. The innocent was not prosecuted and the guilty was not set free. And all this is the result of practising the principle of Identification with the Superior.

Therefore, Motse said : Now, if the rulers and the gentlemen of the world sincerely desire to enrich their country and multiply their people, and to put the government and jurisdiction in order and stabilize the state—if so, then they cannot afford to fail to understand the principle of Identification with the Superior, which is the foundation of government.

instructs an envoy set out on a mission. The two stanzas according to Legge, vol. iv, p. 249, read :

> " My horses are piebald ;
> The six reins are like silk.
> I gallop them and urge them on,
> Everywhere seeking information and counsel.
>
> My horses are white and black-maned ;
> The six reins look glossy.
> I gallop them and urge them on,
> Everywhere seeking information and advice."

CHAPTER XIII

IDENTIFICATION WITH THE SUPERIOR (III)

Motse said : The interest of the wise (ruler) lies in carrying out what makes for order among the people and avoiding what makes for confusion.

But what is it that makes for order among the people ?

When the administration of the ruler answers to the desires of the people there will be order, otherwise there will be confusion.

How do we know it is so ?

When the administration of the ruler answers to the desires of the subjects, it manifests an understanding of the approvals and disapprovals of the people. When there is such an understanding, the good will be discovered and rewarded and the bad will be discovered and punished, and the country will surely have order. When the administration of the ruler does not answer to the desires of the subjects, it shows a lack of understanding of the approvals and disapprovals of the subjects. When there is no such understanding then the good will not be discovered and rewarded and the bad will not be discovered and punished. With the good unrewarded and the evil unpunished, such a government will surely put the country into disorder. Therefore when rewards and punishments do not answer to the desires of the people, the matter has to be carefully looked into.

But how can the desires of the people (being so many and various) be met ?

Therefore Motse said : It can be done only by adopting the principle of Identification with the Superior in government.

How do we know the principle of Identification with the Superior can govern the empire ?

Why not then examine the administration and the theory of government of the ancient times ? In the beginning there was no ruler and everybody was independent. Since every one was independent, there would be one purpose when there was one man, ten purposes when there were ten men, a hundred purposes when there were a hundred men, a thousand purposes when there were a thousand men and so on until the number of men became innumerable and the number of different purposes became innumerable with it. And all of them approved their own ideas and disapproved those of others. And there was strife among the strong and struggle among the weak.

Thereupon Heaven [1] wished to unify the standards in the world. The virtuous was selected and made emperor. Conscious of the insufficiency of his power alone to govern the empire, the emperor chose the next best (in virtue and wisdom) and honoured them to be the three ministers. Conscious of the insufficiency of their powers alone to assist the emperor, the three ministers in turn divided the empire into feudal states and assigned them to feudal lords. Conscious of the insufficiency of his power alone to govern all that were within his four borders, the feudal lord in turn selected his next best and commissioned them ministers and secretaries. Conscious of the insufficiency of their power alone to assist their feudal lord, the ministers and secretaries again selected their next best and appointed them district heads and clan patriarchs.

[1] The subject becomes explicit here while it is omitted in the last two chapters. *Supra,* p. 56, note 1 ; p. 59, note 1.

Therefore, in appointing the three ministers, the feudal lords, the ministers and secretaries, and the district heads and clan patriarchs, the emperor was not selecting them for wealth and honour, leisure and ease. It was to employ them to help in administration and jurisdiction. Hence, when Heaven established the empire and located the capital and commissioned the sovereign, kings, lords, and dukes, and appointed secretaries, scholars, professors, and elders—it was not to give them ease, but only to divide up the task and let them help carry out the light of Heaven.

Why are the superiors now unable to govern their subordinates, and the subordinates unwilling to serve their superiors ? It is because of a mutual disregard.

What is the reason for this ? The reason is a difference in standards. Whenever standards differ there will be opposition. The ruler may think a man good and reward him. The man, though rewarded by the ruler, yet by the same act provokes the condemnation of the people. Therefore those who do good are not necessarily encouraged by rewards. The ruler may think a man evil and punish him. This man, though punished by the ruler, yet at the same time receives the approval of the people. Therefore those who do evil are not necessarily obstructed by punishments. Thus reward and honour from the ruler cannot encourage the good and his denunciation and punishment cannot prevent the evil. What is the reason for this ? The reason is a difference in standards.

But how can the standards in the world be unified ?

Motse said : Why not let each member of the clan organize his purposes and identify them with those of the patriarch ? [1]

[1] The text here is faulty. This reading is suggested internally by the next two parallel paragraphs.

And let the patriarch give laws and proclaim to the clan :
" Whoever discovers a benefactor to the clan shall report it ;
whoever discovers a malefactor to the clan shall report it.
Whoever reports the benefactor of the clan upon seeing
one is equivalent to benefiting the clan himself. Knowing
him the superior will reward him, hearing of him the group
will praise him. Whoever fails to report a malefactor of the
clan upon seeing one is equivalent to doing evil to the clan
himself. Knowing him the superior will punish him, hearing
of him the group will condemn him." Thereupon all the
members of the clan wish to obtain reward and honour and
avoid denunciation and punishment from their superior.
Seeing the good they will report ; seeing the evil they will
report. And the patriarch can reward the good and punish
the evil. With the good rewarded and the evil punished,
the clan will surely have order. Now, why is it that the clan
becomes orderly ? Just because the administration is based
on the principle of Identification with the Superior.

Now that the clan is in order, is that all there is of the way
of governing the feudal state ?

By no means. The state is composed of many clans. They
all like their own clan and dislike other clans. And there is
strife among the strong and struggle among the weak. Therefore the clan patriarchs should again organize the purposes
in the clan and identify them with those of the feudal lord.
The feudal lord also should give laws and should proclaim to
the state : " Whoever discovers a benefactor of the state
shall report it ; whoever discovers a malefactor of the state
shall report it. Whoever reports a benefactor of the state
upon seeing one is equivalent to benefiting the state himself.

Knowing him the superior will reward him, hearing of him the people will praise him. Whoever fails to report a malefactor of the state upon seeing one is equivalent to doing evil to the state himself. Knowing him the superior will punish him, hearing of him the people will condemn him." Thereupon all people in the state wish to obtain reward and honour and avoid denunciation and punishment from their superior. Seeing the good they will report, seeing the evil they will report. And the feudal lord can reward the good and punish the evil. With the good rewarded and the evil punished, the feudal state will surely have order. Now, why is it that the state becomes orderly? Just because the administration is based on the principle of Identification with the Superior.

Now that the feudal state is in order, is that all there is to the way of governing the empire?

By no means. The empire is composed of many states. They all like their own state and dislike other states. And there is strife among the strong and struggle among the weak. Therefore the feudal lord should again organize the purposes in the state and identify them with those of the emperor. The emperor also should give laws and should proclaim to the empire: " Whoever discovers a benefactor of the empire shall report it; whoever discovers a malefactor of the empire shall report it. Whoever reports a benefactor of the empire upon seeing one is equivalent to benefiting the state himself. Knowing him the superior will reward him, hearing of him the people will praise him. Whoever fails to report a malefactor upon seeing one is equivalent to doing evil to the empire himself. Knowing him the superior will punish him, hearing of him the people will condemn him."

Thereupon all the people in the empire will wish to obtain reward and honour and avoid denunciation and punishment from their emperor. Seeing the good and the evil they will report. And the emperor can reward the good and punish the evil. With the good rewarded and the evil punished, the empire will surely have order. Now why is it that the empire becomes orderly? Just because the administration is based on the principle of Identification with the Superior.

Now that the empire becomes orderly, the emperor will further organize the purposes in the empire and identify them with the Will of Heaven.

Therefore Identification with the Superior as a principle can govern the empire when used by the emperor, it can govern the state when used by the feudal lord, and it can govern the clan when used by the clan patriarch. To be found not wanting when used on a large scale to govern the empire, and not useless when employed on a small scale to govern a clan—this is said of such a principle. Hence the proverb: "To govern the world-empire is the same as to rule a single family clan; to command all the people in the world is the same as to order a single individual."

Does any one think that all this is just a fancy of Motse, and that this teaching did not exist among the sage-kings of old? Really they were of the same opinion. All the sage-kings administered their government by the principle of Identification with the Superior, therefore the world became orderly. How do we know it is so? It is recorded in the "Grand Oath" among the books of the ancient kings: "If an unscrupulous man discovers a case of intrigue and deception

and fails to make it known, he shall be punished equally." [1]
This is to say that whoever discovers any crime and does not
report it will be taken as committing a crime of the same
order.

Therefore in governing the empire, the ancient sage-kings
chose only the excellent for the outposts as well as for the
offices near him. As there were many to help him see and
hear, he succeeded before others in planning, and completed
before others in executing, and his good name was spread
before others. Just because he could trust his staff in the
administration, the benefits were as we have stated. There
is an ancient proverb saying : " The sight of one eye cannot
compare with that of two ; the hearing of one ear cannot
compare with that of two ; the grasp of one hand cannot
compare with that of two." Now, just because he could
trust his staff in the administration the sage-king received
such benefits. Therefore during the reign of the ancient
sage-king over the empire, if there was a virtuous man more
than a thousand li away he could reward him before the people
in the same district and village all got to know it. And if
there was a wicked man about a thousand li away he could
punish him before the people in the same district and village
all got to know it. Though it may be supposed that the sage-
king was keen in hearing and sight, how could he see all that
is beyond a thousand li at one look, how could he hear all that
is beyond a thousand li at one hearing ? In fact the sage-
king could see without going there and hear without being

---

[1] In the present text of *Shu Ching* this quotation does not appear. Only
the last clause with some modification is found in the "Grand Oath".
Cf. Legge, vol. iii, p. 287.

near. Yet what kept the thieves, robbers, bandits, and high-waymen moving all over the empire without being able to find refuge anywhere ?   There is the beauty of adopting the principle of Identification with the Superior in government.

Therefore Motse said : Whoever orders his people to identify themselves with their superior must love them dearly. For the people will not obey orders except when they are ordered with love and held in confidence.   Lead them with wealth and honour ahead, and push them with just punishments from behind.   When government is carried on like this, even though I wanted to have some one not to identify himself with me, it would be impossible.

Therefore Motse said : If the kings, dukes, and important personages of the world now sincerely want to practise magnanimity and righteousness and be superior men, if they want to attain the way of the sage-kings on the one hand and contribute toward the benefit of the people on the other, they cannot leave the principle of Identification with the Superior unexamined and un-understood. Identification with the Superior is, indeed, the foundation of government and essence of orderliness.

BOOK IV

CHAPTER XIV

Universal Love (I) [1]

The wise man who has charge of governing the empire should know the cause of disorder before he can put it in order. Unless he knows its cause, he cannot regulate it. It is similar to the problem of a physician who is attending a patient. He has to know the cause of the ailment before he can cure it. Unless he knows its cause he cannot cure it. How is the situation different for him who is to regulate disorder ? He too has to know the cause of the disorder before he can regulate it. Unless he knows its cause he cannot regulate it. The wise man who has charge of governing the empire must, then, investigate the cause of disorder.

Suppose we try to locate the cause of disorder, we shall find it lies in the want of mutual love. What is called disorder is just the lack of filial piety on the part of the minister and the son towards the emperor and the father. As he loves himself and not his father the son benefits himself to the disadvantage of his father. As he loves himself and not his elder brother, the younger brother benefits himself to the disadvantage of his elder brother. As he loves himself and not his emperor, the minister benefits himself to the

---

[1] This chapter has been translated by Legge in his Prolegomena to *Mencius* 孟 子, *Chinese Classics*, vol. ii. His translation is based on Pi Yuan edition of the text which is inferior to Sun Yi Jang, and his own reading of that edition is also incorrect on a few points.

disadvantage of his emperor. And these are what is called disorder. When the father shows no affection to the son, when the elder brother shows no affection to the younger brother, and when the emperor shows no affection to the minister, on the other hand, it is also called disorder. When the father loves only himself and not the son, he benefits himself to the disadvantage of the son. When the elder brother loves only himself and not his younger brother, he benefits himself to the disadvantage of the younger brother. When the emperor loves only himself and not his minister, he benefits himself to the disadvantage of his minister, and the reason for all these is want of mutual love.

This is true even among thieves and robbers. As he loves only his own family and not other families, the thief steals from other families to profit his own family. As he loves only his own person and not others, the robber does violence to others to profit himself. And the reason for all this is want of love. This again is true in the mutual disturbance among the houses of the ministers and the mutual invasions among the states of the feudal lords. As he loves only his own house and not the others, the minister disturbs the other houses to profit his own. As he loves only his own state and not the others, the feudal lord attacks the other states to profit his own. These instances exhaust the confusion in the world. And when we look into the causes we find they all arise from want of mutual love.

Suppose everybody in the world loves universally, loving others as one's self. Will there yet be any unfilial individual ? When every one regards his father, elder brother, and emperor as himself, whereto can he direct any unfilial feeling ? Will

there still be any unaffectionate individual ? When every
one regards his younger brother, son, and minister as himself,
whereto can he direct any disaffection ? Therefore there
will not be any unfilial feeling or disaffection. Will there
then be any thieves and robbers ? When every one regards
other families as his own family, who will steal ? When
every one regards other persons as his own person, who will
rob ? Therefore there will not be any thieves or robbers.
Will there be mutual disturbance among the houses of the
ministers and invasion among the states of the feudal lords ?
When every one regards the houses of others as one's own,
who will be disturbing ? When every one regards the states
of others as one's own, who will invade ? Therefore there will
be neither disturbances among the houses of the ministers nor
invasion among the states of the feudal lords.

If every one in the world will love universally ; states
not attacking one another ; houses not disturbing one
another ; thieves and robbers becoming extinct ; emperor
and ministers, fathers and sons, all being affectionate and
filial—if all this comes to pass the world will be orderly.
Therefore, how can the wise man who has charge of governing
the empire fail to restrain hate and encourage love ? So,
when there is universal love in the world it will be orderly,
and when there is mutual hate in the world it will be disorderly. This is why Motse insisted on persuading people
to love others.

CHAPTER XV

UNIVERSAL LOVE (II)

Motse said : The purpose of the magnanimous is to be found in procuring benefits for the world and eliminating its calamities.

But what are the benefits of the world and what its calamities ?

Motse said : Mutual attacks among states, mutual usurpation among houses, mutual injuries among individuals ; the lack of grace and loyalty between ruler and ruled, the lack of affection and filial piety between father and son, the lack of harmony between elder and younger brothers— these are the major calamities in the world.

But whence did these calamities arise, out of mutual love ?

Motse said : They arise out of want of mutual love. At present feudal lords have learned only to love their own states and not those of others. Therefore they do not scruple about attacking other states. The heads of houses have learned only to love their own houses and not those of others. Therefore they do not scruple about usurping other houses. And individuals have learned only to love themselves and not others. Therefore they do not scruple about injuring others. When feudal lords do not love one another there will be war on the fields. When heads of houses do not love one another they will usurp one another's power. When individuals do not love one another they will injure one another. When ruler and ruled do not love one another they will not be gracious and loyal. When father and son do not love each other they will not be affectionate and filial. When elder and younger brothers do not love each other they will not be harmonious. When nobody in the world loves any other, naturally the strong will overpower the weak, the many will oppress the few, the wealthy will mock the poor, the honoured will disdain the humble, the cunning will deceive the simple. Therefore all the calamities, strifes, complaints, and hatred in the world have arisen out of want of mutual love. Therefore the benevolent disapproved of this want.

Now that there is disapproval, how can we have the condition altered ?

Motse said it is to be altered by the way of universal love and mutual aid.

But what is the way of universal love and mutual aid ?

Motse said : It is to regard the state of others as one's own, the houses of others as one's own, the persons of others as one's self. When feudal lords love one another there will be no more war ; when heads of houses love one another there will be no more mutual usurpation ; when individuals love one another there will be no more mutual injury. When ruler and ruled love each other they will be gracious and loyal ; when father and son love each other they will be affectionate and filial ; when elder and younger brothers love each other they will be harmonious. When all the people in the world love one another, then the strong will not overpower the weak, the many will not oppress the few, the wealthy will not mock the poor, the honoured will not disdain the humble, and the cunning will not deceive the simple. And it is all due to mutual love that calamities, strifes, complaints, and hatred are prevented from arising. Therefore the benevolent exalt it.

But the gentlemen of the world would say : " So far so good. It is of course very excellent when love becomes universal. But it is only a difficult and distant ideal."

Motse said : This is simply because the gentlemen of the world do not recognize what is to the benefit of the world, or understand what is its calamity. Now, to besiege a city, to fight in the fields, or to achieve a name at the cost of death—these are what men find difficult. Yet when the superior encourages them, the multitude can do them. Besides, universal love and mutual aid is quite different from these. Whoever loves others is loved by others ; whoever benefits others is benefited by others ; whoever hates others is hated by others ; whoever injures others is injured by others. Then, what difficulty is there with it (universal love) ? Only, the ruler fails to embody it in his government and the ordinary man in his conduct.

Formerly, Lord Wen of the state of Chin (about 630 B.C.) liked the uncouth uniform of the soldier. And so all his ministers and officers wore sheepskin jackets, carried their swords in leather girdles, and put on silk-spun hats.[1] Thus attired, they attended the Lord when they went in and paced the court when they stayed out. What was the reason for this ? It was that what the ruler encourages the ruled will carry out. And Lord Ling of the state of Ch'u (about 535 B.C.) liked slender waists. And so all his ministers and

---

[1] These hats were considered very plain and unbecoming to men of high position. Cotton is cheaper than silk to-day, but was not introduced into China until many centuries later.

officers limited themselves to a single meal (a day). They tied their belts after exhaling, and could not stand up without leaning against the wall. Within a year the court looked grim and dark. What was the reason for this ? It was that what the ruler encourages the ruled will carry out. Again, Lord Kou Chien of the state of Yüeh (about 480 B.C.) liked the warrior's courage, and trained his subjects accordingly. He had his palace boat set on fire. To test his soldiers he proclaimed that all the treasures of the state were contained therein. And he beat the drum himself to urge them on. Hearing the drum the soldiers rushed on in disorder. More than a hundred strong perished in the flames. Thereupon the Lord beat the gong to let them retreat.

Therefore Motse said : Now, things like scantily died coarse clothing and the achievement of a name at the cost of death are those in which people find difficulty. Yet when the ruler encourages them the multitude can stand them. Besides, universal love and mutual aid are different from these. Whoever loves others is loved by others ; whoever benefits others is benefited by others ; whoever hates others is hated by others ; whoever injures others is injured by others. Then what difficulty is there with it (universal love) ? Only, the ruler fails to embody it in his government and the ordinary man in his conduct.

Nevertheless, the gentlemen in the empire think that, though it would be an excellent thing if love can be universalized, it is something quite impracticable. It is like carrying Mt. T'ai and leaping over the Chi River.

Motse said : The illustration is a faulty one. Of course

to be able to carry Mt. T'ai and leap over the Chi River would be an extreme feat of strength. Such has never been performed from antiquity to the present time. But universal love and mutual aid are quite different from this. And the ancient sage-kings did practise it. How do we know they did ? When Yü was working to bring the Deluge under control, he dug the West River and the Yu Tou River in the west in order to let off the water from the Ch'ü, Sun, and Huang Rivers. In the north he built a dam across the Yuan and Ku Rivers in order to fill the Hou Chih Ti (a basin) and the Hu Ch'ih River. Mt. Ti Chu was made use of as a water divide, and a tunnel was dug through Mt. Lung Men. All these were done to benefit the peoples west of the (Yellow) River and various barbarian tribes, Yen, Tai, Hu, Ho, of the north. In the east he drained the great Plain and built dykes along the Meng Chu River. The watercourse was divided into nine canals in order to regulate the water in the east and in order to benefit the people of the District of Chi.[1] In the south he completed the Yangtze, Han, Huai, and Ju Rivers. These ran eastward and emptied themselves into the Five Lakes. This was done in order to benefit the peoples of Ching, Ch'u, Kan, Yüeh, and the barbarians of the south. All these are the deeds of Yü. We can, then, universalize love in conduct.

When King Wen was ruling the Western land, he shone forth like the sun and the moon all over the four quarters as well as in the Western land. He did not allow the big state to oppress the small state, he did not allow the multitude to oppress the single-handed, he did not allow the influential

---

[1] China proper at that time.

and strong to take away the grain and live stock from the farmers. Heaven visited him with blessing. And, therefore, the old and childless had the wherewithal to spend their old age, the solitary and brotherless had the opportunity to join in the social life of men, and the orphans had the support for their growth. This was what King Wen had accomplished. We can, then, universalize love in conduct.

When King Wu was about to do service to Mt. T'ai it was recorded thus : " Blessed is Mt. T'ai. Duke of Chou by a long descent is about to perform his duty. As I have obtained the approval of Heaven, the magnanimous arise to save the people of Shang Hsia [1] as well as the barbarians (from the tyranny of Emperor Chow). Though (Emperor Chow) has many near relatives, they cannot compare with the magnanimous. If there is sin anywhere, I am solely responsible." [2] This relates the deeds of King Wu. We can, then, universalize love in conduct.

Therefore Motse said : If the rulers sincerely desire the empire to be wealthy and dislike to have it poor, desire to have it orderly and dislike to have it chaotic, they should bring about universal love and mutual aid. This is the way of the sage-kings and the way to order for the world, and it should not be neglected.

---

[1] Hsia is one of the eulogistic names for the Chinese or China. Shang Hsia, then, means China under the Shang Dynasty.

[2] This quotation as a whole is not found in any of the existing texts of the classics. The last two sentences are found in the " Great Declaration " in *Shu Ching*. Legge gives a different meaning to the last sentence. A passage in " The Successful Completion of the War " shows some resemblance to the first part of the quotation. But this essay is one of the most noted for falsifications in the whole collection of *Shu Ching*. The references to Legge are vol. iii, part ii, p. 292 and pp. 312-13.

CHAPTER XVI

Universal Love (III)

Motse said : The purpose of the magnanimous lies in procuring benefits for the world and eliminating its calamities. Now among all the current calamities, which are the most important ? The attack on the small states by the large ones, disturbances of the small houses by the large ones, oppression of the weak by the strong, misuse of the few by the many, deception of the simple by the cunning, disdain towards the humble by the honoured—these are the misfortunes in the empire. Again, the lack of grace on the part of the ruler, the lack of loyalty on the part of the ruled, the lack of affection on the part of the father, the lack of filial piety on the part of the son—these are further calamities in the empire. Also, the mutual injury and harm which the unscrupulous do to one another with weapons, poison, water, and fire is still another calamity in the empire.

When we come to think about the cause of all these calamities, how have they arisen ? Have they arisen out of love of others and benefiting others ? Of course we should say no. We should say they have arisen out of hate of others and injuring others. If we should classify one by one all those who hate others and injure others, should we find them to be universal in love or partial ? Of course we should say they are partial. Now, since partiality against one another is the cause of the major calamities in the empire, then partiality is wrong.

Motse continued : Whoever criticizes others must have

something to replace them. Criticism without suggestion is like trying to stop flood with flood and put out fire with fire. It will surely be without worth.

Motse said : Partiality is to be replaced by universality. But how is it that partiality can be replaced by universality ? Now, when every one regards the states of others as he regards his own, who would attack the others' states ? Others are regarded like self. When every one regards the capitals of others as he regards his own, who would seize the others' capitals ? Others are regarded like self. When every one regards the houses of others as he regards his own, who would disturb the others' houses ? Others are regarded like self. Now, when the states and cities do not attack and seize each other and when the clans and individuals do not disturb and harm one another—is this a calamity or a benefit to the world ? Of course it is a benefit. When we come to think about the several benefits in regard to their cause, how have they arisen ? Have they arisen out of hate of others and injuring others ? Of course we should say no. We should say they have arisen out of love of others and benefiting others. If we should classify one by one all those who love others and benefit others, should we find them to be partial or universal ? Of course we should say they are universal. Now, since universal love is the cause of the major benefits in the world, therefore Motse proclaims universal love is right.

And, as has already been said, the interest of the magnanimous lies in procuring benefits for the world and eliminating its calamities. Now that we have found out the consequences of universal love to be the major benefits of the world and

the consequences of partiality to be the major calamities
in the world ; this is the reason why Motse said partiality
is wrong and universality is right. When we try to develop
and procure benefits for the world with universal love as
our standard, then attentive ears and keen eyes will respond
in service to one another, then limbs will be strengthened
to work for one another, and those who know the Tao will
untiringly instruct others. Thus the old and those who have
neither wife nor children will have the support and supply
to spend their old age with, and the young and weak and
orphans will have the care and admonition to grow up in.
When universal love is adopted as the standard, then such
are the consequent benefits. It is incomprehensible, then,
why people should object to universal love when they
hear it.

Yet the objection is not all exhausted. It is asked : " It
may be a good thing, but can it be of any use ? "

Motse replied : If it were not useful then even I would
disapprove of it. But how can there be anything that is
good but not useful ? Let us consider the matter from both
sides. Suppose there are two men. Let one of them hold
to partiality and the other to universality. Then the
advocate of partiality would say to himself, how can I take
care of my friend as I do of myself, how can I take care of
his parents as my own ? Therefore when he finds his friend
hungry he would not feed him, and when he finds him cold
he would not clothe him. In his illness he would not minister
to him, and when he is dead he would not bury him. Such is
the word and such is the deed of the advocate of partiality.
The advocate of universality is quite unlike this both in word

and in deed. He would say to himself, I have heard that to be a superior man one should take care of his friend as he does of himself, and take care of his friend's parents as his own. Therefore when he finds his friend hungry he would feed him, and when he finds him cold he would clothe him. In his sickness he would serve him, and when he is dead he would bury him. Such is the word and such is the deed of the advocate of universality.

These two persons then are opposed to each other in word and also in deed. Suppose they are sincere in word and decisive in deed so that their word and deed are made to agree like the two parts of a tally, and that there is no word but what is realized in deed, then let us consider further: Suppose a war is on, and one is in armour and helmet ready to join the force, life and death are not predictable. Or suppose one is commissioned a deputy by the ruler to such far countries like Pa, Yüeh, Ch'i, and Ching, and the arrival and return are quite uncertain. Now (under such circumstances) let us inquire upon whom would one lay the trust of one's family and parents. Would it be upon the universal friend or upon the partial friend ? It seems to me, on occasions like these, there are no fools in the world. Even if he is a person who objects to universal love, he will lay the trust upon the universal friend all the same. This is verbal objection to the principle but actual selection by it — this is self-contradiction between one's word and deed. It is incomprehensible, then, why people should object to universal love when they hear it.

Yet the objection is not all exhausted. It is objected:

Maybe it is a good criterion to choose among ordinary men, but it may not apply to the rulers.

Let us again consider the matter from both sides. Suppose there are two rulers. Let one of them hold partiality and the other universality. Then the partial ruler would say to himself, how can I take care of the people as I do of myself? This would be quite contrary to common sense. A man's life on earth is of short duration, it is like a galloping horse passing by. Therefore when he finds his people hungry he would not feed them, and when he finds them cold he would not clothe them. When they are sick he would not minister to them, and upon their death he would not bury them. Such is the word and such is the deed of the partial ruler. The universal ruler is quite unlike this both in word and in deed. He would say to himself, I have heard that to be an upright ruler of the world one should first attend to his people and then to himself. Therefore when he finds his people hungry he would feed them, and when he finds them cold he would clothe them. In their sickness he would minister to them, and upon their death he would bury them. Such is the word and such is the deed of the universal ruler.

These two rulers, then, are opposed to each other in word and also in deed. Suppose they are sincere in word and decisive in deed so that their word and deed are made to agree like the two parts of a tally, and that there is no word but what is realized in deed, then let us consider further: Suppose, now, that there is a disastrous pestilence, that most people are in misery and privation, and that many lie dead in ditches.[1] (Under such circumstances) let us inquire, if a person could choose one of the two rulers, which would he prefer ? It seems to me on such occasions there are no fools in the world. Even if he is a person who objects to universal love, he will choose the universal ruler. This is verbal objection to the principle but actual selection by it—this is self-contradiction between one's word and deed. It is incomprehensible, then, why people should object to universal love when they hear it.

Yet the objection is still not exhausted. It points out that universal love may be magnanimous and righteous, but how can it be realized ? Universal love is impracticable just as carrying Mt. T'ai and leaping over rivers. So, then, universal love is but a pious wish, how can it be actualized ?

Motse replied : To carry Mt. T'ai and leap over rivers is something that has never been accomplished since the existence of man. But universal love and mutual aid has been personally practised by six ancient sage-kings.

How do we know they have done it ?

Motse said : I am no contemporary of theirs, neither have I heard their voice or seen their faces. The sources of our knowledge lie in what is written on the bamboos and silk, what is engraved in metal and stones, and what is cut in the vessels to be handed down to posterity.[2]

The " Great Declaration " proclaims : " King Wen was like the sun and the moon, shedding glorious and resplendent light in the four quarters as well as over the Western land."

---

[1] That is, without means to be buried in tombs. To have the dead properly buried is a major duty of the son and the ruler of the dead person.

[2] *Supra*, p. 51, notes 1 and 2.

This is to say that the love of King Wen is so wide and universal that it is like the sun and the moon shining upon the world without partiality. Here is universal love on the part of King Wen; what Motse has been talking about is really derived from the example of King Wen.

Moreover it is true not only in the " Great Declaration ", but also with the " Oath of Yü ".[1] Yü said (therein) : " Come all you hosts of people, take heed and hearken to my words. It is not that I, a single person, would willingly stir up this confusion. The Prince of Miao is more and more unreasonable, he deserves punishment from Heaven. There-fore I lead you to appoint the lords of the states and go to punish the Prince of Miao." It was not for the sake of increasing his wealth and multiplying his felicitations and indulging his ears and eyes but for that of procuring benefits for the world and eliminating its annoyances that Yü went to war against the Prince of Miao. This is universal love on the part of Yü, and what Motse has been talking about is really derived from the example of Yü.

Again it is true not only in the " Oath of Yü " but also with the " Oath of T'ang ". T'ang said : " Unworthy Lü presumed to do sacrifice with a first-born male animal to Heaven on high and mother Earth, saying, ' Now there is a great drought from heaven. It happens right in my, Lü's, time. I do not know whether I have wronged Heaven or men. Good, I dare not cover up ; guilt, I dare not let go— this is clearly seen in the mind of God. If there is sin

---

[1] This title does not appear in the present text of *Shu Ching*. Something similar to the content of the following quotation is found in the " Counsels of Yü ". Cf. Legge, vol. iii, pp. 64, 65.

anywhere hold me responsible for it ; if I myself am guilty
may the rest be spared.' " [1]   This is to say that though having
the honour of being an emperor and the wealth of possessing
the whole world, T'ang did not shrink from offering himself
as sacrifice to implore God and the spirits.   This is universal
love on the part of T'ang, and what Motse has been talking
about is really derived from the example of T'ang.

Still again, it is true not only in the " Oath of Yü " and
the " Oath of T'ang " but also with the " Poems of Chou ".[2]
To quote : " the way of the (good) emperor is wide and
straight, without partiality and without favouritism.   The
way of the (good) emperor is even and smooth, without
favouritism and without partiality.   It is straight like an
arrow and just like a balance.   The superior man follows it,
(even) the unprincipled looks on (without resentment)."
Thus the principle that I have been expounding is not to be
regarded as a mere doctrinaire notion.   In the past, when
Wen and Wu administered the government both of them
rewarded the virtuous and punished the wicked without
partiality to their relatives and brothers.   This is just the
universal love of Wen and Wu.   And what Motse has been
talking about is really derived from the examples of Wen
and Wu.[3]   It is incomprehensible then why people should
object to universal love when they hear it.

[1] The passage is not found in the " Oath of T'ang ".   The several
sentences are scattered through the " Announcement of T'ang " in
Shu Ching. Cf. Legge, vol. iii, pp. 184–90.

[2] This reference leads us to look for the quotation in *Shih Ching.*
But it is not there.   The first two sentences appear in the " Great Plan "
in *Shu Ching.* Legge, vol. iii, p. 331.

[3] Altogether four ancient kings, Yü, T'ang, Wen, and Wu, are cited.   The
word " six " in the introductory paragraph, p. 92, to this section seems
to be due to the oversight of some copyist.

Yet the objection is still not exhausted. It raises the question, when one does not think in terms of benefits and harm to one's parents would it be filial piety ?

Motse replied : Now let us inquire about the plans of the filial sons for their parents. I may ask, when they plan for their parents, whether they desire to have others love or hate them ? Judging from the whole doctrine (of filial piety), it is certain that they desire to have others love their parents. Now, what should I do first in order to attain this ? Should I first love others' parents in order that they would love my parents in return, or should I first hate others' parents in order that they would love my parents in return ? Of course I should first love others' parents in order that they would love my parents in return. Hence those who desire to be filial to one another's parents, if they have to choose (between whether they should love or hate others' parents), had best first love and benefit others' parents. Would any one suspect that all the filial sons are stupid and incorrigible (in loving their own parents) ? We may again inquire about it. It is said in the " Ta Ya " [1] among the books of the ancient kings : " No idea is not given its due value ; no virtue is not rewarded. When a peach is thrown to us, we would return with a prune." This is to say whoever loves others will be loved and whoever hates others will be hated. It is then quite incomprehensible why people should object to universal love when they hear it.

Is it because it is hard and impracticable ? There are

---

[1] " Ta Ya " is the name of a group of odes in *Shih Ching*. Only the first two lines of the following quotation appear in the ode " Yi ". Legge, vol. iv, p. 514, renders it :

> " Every word finds its answer ;
> Every good deed has its recompense."

instances of even much harder tasks done. Formerly, Lord
Ling of the state of Ching [1] liked slender waists. In his time
people in the state of Ching ate not more than once a day.
They could not stand up without support, and could not walk
without leaning against the wall. Now, limited diet is quite
hard to endure, and yet it was endured. While Lord Ling
encouraged it, his people could be changed within a generation
to conform to their superior. Lord Kou Chien of the state
of Yüeh admired courage and taught it his ministers and
soldiers three years. Fearing that their knowledge had not
yet made them efficient he let a fire be set on the boat, and
beat the drum to signal advance. The soldiers at the head
of the rank were even pushed down. Those who perished in
the flames and in water were numberless. Even then they
would not retreat without signal. The soldiers of Yüeh
would be quite terrified (ordinarily). To be burnt alive is
a hard task, and yet it was accomplished. When the Lord
of Yüeh encouraged it, his people could be changed within
a generation to conform to their superior. Lord Wen of
the state of Chin liked coarse clothing. And so in his time
the people of Chin wore suits of plain cloth, jackets of sheep
skin, hats of spun silk, and big rough shoes. Thus attired,
they would go in and see the Lord and come out and walk
in the court. To dress up in coarse clothing is hard to do,
yet it has been done. When Lord Wen encouraged it his
people could be changed within a generation to conform to
their superior.

Now to endure limited diet, to be burnt alive, and to

[1] Ching and Ch'u are names of the same state at this time. In chap. xv,
p. 83, Ch'u is used.

wear coarse clothing are the hardest things in the world, yet when the superiors encouraged them the people could be changed within a generation. Why was this so ? It was due to the desire to conform to the superior. Now, as to universal love and mutual aid, they are beneficial and easy beyond a doubt. It seems to me that the only trouble is that there is no superior who encourages it. If there is a superior who encourages it, promoting it with rewards and commendations, threatening its reverse with punishments, I feel people will tend toward universal love and mutual aid like fire tending upward and water downwards—it will be unpreventable in the world.

Therefore, universal love is really the way of the sage-kings. It is what gives peace to the rulers and sustenance to the people. The gentleman would do well to understand and practise universal love ; then he would be gracious as a ruler, loyal as a minister, affectionate as a father, filial as a son, courteous as an elder brother, and respectful as a younger brother. So, if the gentleman desires to be a gracious ruler, a loyal minister, an affectionate father, a filial son, a courteous elder brother, and a respectful younger brother,[1] universal love must be practised. It is the way of the sage-kings and the great blessing of the people.

[1] Through the entire treatment of universal love, and especially in this summary at the end, the Western reader must be missing some consideration of the relation between husband and wife, mother and child. Mother is not specified because in parental affection she enjoys absolute equality with the father. Husband and wife constitute another of the five cardinal relations in Chinese society. But that relation has seldom been dwelt on in the whole body of literature, because the Chinese shares with his fellow-Orientals in a sense of restraint about such natural and socio-biological matters. The author is perhaps also conscious that that relation will take care of itself when the others all follow the principle of universal love.

BOOK V

CHAPTER XVII

CONDEMNATION OF OFFENSIVE WAR (I) [1]

Suppose a man enters the orchard of another and steals the other's peaches and plums. Hearing of it the public will condemn it; laying hold of him the authorities will punish him. Why? Because he injures others to profit himself. As to seizing dogs, pigs, chickens, and young pigs from another, it is even more unrighteous than to steal peaches and plums from his orchard. Why? Because it causes others to suffer more,[2] and it is more inhumane and criminal. When it comes to entering another's stable and appropriating the other's horses and oxen, it is more inhumane than to seize the dogs, pigs, chickens, and young pigs of another. Why? Because others are caused to suffer more; when others are caused to suffer more, then the act is more inhumane and criminal. Finally, as to murdering the innocent, stripping him of his clothing, dispossessing him of his spear and sword, it is even more unrighteous than to enter another's stable and appropriate his horses and oxen. Why? Because it

---

[1] This chapter is quoted in translation in entirety by Professor Hu Shih in his *The Development of the Logical Method in Ancient China*, pp. 69–71. There is hardly any difference between that translation and this one except some instances of choice of words and expressions. The reader may go to that reference for more detailed comparison.

[2] A clause seems to have been lost here, when we compare this sentence with the following sentences expressing the same meaning. The correct text here seems also to be, "Because others are caused to suffer more; when others are caused to suffer more, it is more inhumane and criminal."

causes others to suffer more ; when others are caused to suffer more, then the act is more inhumane and criminal.

All the gentlemen of the world know that they should condemn these things, calling them unrighteous. But when it comes to the great attack of states,[1] they do not know that they should condemn it. On the contrary, they applaud it, calling it righteous. Can this be said to be knowing the difference between righteousness and unrighteousness ?

The murder of one person is called unrighteous and incurs one death penalty. Following this argument, the murder of ten persons will be ten times as unrighteous and there should be ten death penalties ; the murder of a hundred persons will be a hundred times as unrighteous and there should be a hundred death penalties. All the gentlemen of the world know that they should condemn these things, calling them unrighteous. But when it comes to the great unrighteousness of attacking states, they do not know that they should condemn it. On the contrary, they applaud it, calling it righteous. And they are really ignorant of its being unrighteous. Hence they have recorded their judgment to bequeath to their posterity. If they did know that it is unrighteous, then why would they record their false judgment to bequeath to posterity ?

Now, if there were a man who, upon seeing a little blackness, should say it is black, but, upon seeing much, should say it is white ; then we should think he could not tell the difference between black and white. If, upon tasting a little bitterness one should say it is bitter, but, upon tasting much, should

---

[1] A few words seem to have been lost in this clause. The correct text seems to be : " The great unrighteousness of attacking states."

say it is sweet; then we should think he could not tell the difference between bitter and sweet. Now, when a little wrong is committed people know that they should condemn it, but when such a great wrong as attacking a state is committed people do not know that they should condemn it. On the contrary, it is applauded, called righteous. Can this be said to be knowing the difference between the righteous and the unrighteous? Hence we know the gentlemen of the world are confused about the difference between righteousness and unrighteousness.

CHAPTER XVIII

Condemnation of Offensive War (II)

Motse said : If the rulers of to-day sincerely wish to be careful in condemnation and commendation, judicious in rewards and punishments, and temperate in government and jurisdiction ; [1] . . .

Therefore Motse said : There is an ancient saying that, when one is not successful in making out plans then predict the future by the past [2] and learn about the absent from what is present. When one plans like this then one can be intelligent. [3]

Now, about a country going to war. If it is in winter it will be too cold ; if it is in summer it will be too hot. So it should be neither in winter nor in summer. If it is in spring it will take people away from sowing and planting ; if it is in autumn it will take people away from reaping and harvesting. [4] Should they be taken away in either of these seasons, innumerable people would die of hunger and cold. And, when the army sets out, the bamboo arrows, the feather flags, the house tents, the armour, the shields, the sword hilts—innumerable quantities of these will break and rot and never come back. The spears, the lances, the swords,

---

[1] The text of this paragraph is incomplete. The lost clause seems to run somewhat like this : " They must condemn offensive wars." *Infra,* p. 104.

[2] The same idea is expounded in a passage in the Confucian *Analects* 論 語. Cf. Legge, vol. i, book i, p. 8.

[3] This paragraph is an introduction to the historical argument which forms the main body of this chapter.

[4] Following this it seems there should be the sentence : " So it should be neither in spring nor in autumn."

the poniards, the chariots, the carts—innumerable quantities
of these will break and rot and never come back. Then
innumerable horses and oxen will start out fat and come back
lean or will not return at all. And innumerable people will
die because their food will be cut off and cannot be supplied
on account of the great distances of the roads. And
innumerable people will be sick and die of the constant
danger and the irregularity of eating and drinking and the
extremes of hunger and over-eating. Then, the army will be
lost in large numbers or entirely ; in either case the number
will be innumerable. And this means the spirits will lose
their worshippers, and the number of these will also be
innumerable.

Why then does the government deprive the people of
their opportunities and benefits to such a great extent ?
It has been answered : " I covet the fame of the victor and
the possessions obtainable through the conquest. So I
do it."

Motse said : But when we consider the victory as such,
there is nothing useful about it. When we consider the
possessions obtained through it, it does not even make up
for the loss. Now about the siege of a city of three li or a
kuo [1] of seven li—if these could be obtained without the use of
weapons or the killing of lives, it would be all right. But
(as a matter of fact) those killed must be counted by the ten
thousand, those widowed or left solitary must be counted by
the thousand, before a city of three li or a kuo of seven li

---

[1] All Chinese cities until very recently were walled in for protection.
The inner wall is called " ch'eng " 城, city, or city wall, and the outer
wall is called " kuo " 郭.

could be captured. Moreover the states of ten thousand chariots [1] now have empty towns to be counted by the thousand, which can be entered without conquest ; and their extensive lands to be counted by the ten thousand (of mu),[2] which can be cultivated without conquest. So, land is abundant but people are few. Now to pursue the people to death and aggravate the danger feared by both superiors and subordinates in order to obtain an empty city—this is to give up what is needed and to treasure what is already in abundance. Such an undertaking is not in accordance with the interest of the country.

Those who endeavour to gloss over offensive wars would say : " In the south there are the lords of Ching and Yüeh, and in the north there are the lords of Ch'i and Chin. When their states were first assigned to them, they were but a hundred li square in area, and but a few tens of thousands in number of people. By means of wars and attacks, their areas have increased to several thousand li square and the people to several million. So, then, offensive wars are not to be condemned."

Motse said : The four or five states may have reaped their benefits, still it is not conduct according to the Tao.[3] It is like the physician giving his drugs to the patients. If a physician should give all the sick in the world a uniform drug, among the ten thousand who took it there might be four or five who were benefited, still it is not to be said to

---

[1] The size and power of a state were then symbolized by the size of its chariot force. The states that Motse here had in mind are Ch'i, Chin, Ch'u, and Yüeh. *Infra*, chapter xix, pp. 110 and 114.

[2] A "mu" 畝 = ⅛ acre.

[3] That is, the correct way, the universal way.

be a common (commonly beneficial) medicine. Thus a filial son will not give it to his parent and a loyal minister will not give it to his king.[1] After the empire was in the ancient time divided into states a great many of them died of attacks —the earlier cases we hear of through the ear, the recent cases we saw by the eye. How do we know it is so? In the east there was the state of Chü. It was a small state situated in the midst of big states. It did not show respect and obedience to the big states, and the latter therefore did not like it or favour it. So, on the east Yüeh cut and appropriated its land by force, and from the west Ch'i swallowed it up altogether. And it was due to offensive wars that Chü died between two big states. And it was due to offensive war too that in the south Ch'en and Ts'ai were extinguished by Wu and Yüeh. And it was also due to offensive wars that in the north Pu T'u Ho perished among Yen, Tai, Hu and Mo.

Therefore Motse said: If the rulers now really desire gain and avert loss, desire security and avert danger, they cannot but condemn offensive wars.

Those who endeavour to gloss over offensive wars would say: "These states perished because they could not gather and employ their multitudes. I can gather and employ my multitudes and wage war with them; who, then, dare to be unsubmissive?"

Motse said: You might be able to gather and employ your

---

[1] This illustration incidentally reveals the trial and error stage of medical practice at the time. Shen Nung, twenty-eighth century B.C., is said to have tasted the various herbs himself to ascertain their nature. And he is still the patron God of the medical profession in China.

multitudes, but can you compare yourself with the ancient
Ho Lü of Wu ?   Ho Lü of Wu (about 510 B.C.) in the ancient
days drilled his soldiers seven years.   With armour on and
weapons in hand they could cover three hundred li (in a day)
before encamping (for the night).   Passing Chu Lin, they
emerged at the narrow Pass of Min.   They engaged in battle
(with the state of Ch'u) at Po Chü.   Subduing Ch'u, (Ho Lü)
gave audience to Sung and Lu.   By the time of Fu Ch'ai,[1]
he attacked Ch'i in the north, encamped on the Wen River,
fought at Ai Ling and greatly defeated Ch'i and compelled
surety from them at Mt. T'ai.   In the east he attacked Yüeh,
crossing the Three Rivers and the Five Lakes, and compelled
surety at Kuei Chi.   None of the nine tribes dared to show
disrespect.   Reaching home, however, he would not reward
the orphaned or give to the numerous rustics.   He depended
on his own might, gloated over his success, praised his
own cleverness, and neglected instructing and training his
people.   He built the Monument of Ku Su [2] which was not
completed even in seven years.   By this time (the people
of Wu) felt tired and disheartened.   Seeing the friction
between the superior and the subordinates in Wu, Kou
Chien of Yüeh gathered his multitudes to take revenge.   He
broke into its kuo on the north, moved away its royal boat,
and surrounded its palace.   And thus Wu perished.

Some time ago Chin had six ministers and Chih Po (about
455 B.C.) was the most powerful.   He considered the large
area of his land and the great number of his people, and
desired to attack the feudal lords in order to have a rapid

---

[1] Ho Lü's son (about 490 B.C.).

[2] Capital of the state of Wu, now Soochow.

spread of his courageous name through war and battle. So he ranked his brave warriors and arranged his boat and chariot forces. He attacked (the house of) Chung Hsing and seized it. This showed to him that his plans were satisfactory. Then he attacked Fan and totally defeated him. Thus he absorbed three families into one. He did not stop even there, but surrounded Minister Hsiang of Chao at Chin Yang. By this time Han and Wei came together and deliberated, saying : " An ancient proverb says : ' When the lips are removed the teeth will become cold.' The house of Chao dying in the morning we would be following it in the evening ; the house of Chao dying in the evening we would be following it in the morning. A poet sings : ' If the fish would not act while yet in water, what can it do when it is already placed on land ? ' " Thereupon the three ministers worked with united strength and a single mind, opening passes and blazing trails, putting on armour and arousing the warriors. With Han and Wei from without and Chao from within, they battled Chih Po and totally defeated him.

Therefore Motse said : An ancient proverb says : " The superior man would not go to water but to man for a mirror.[1] In water as a mirror one sees only one's face ; in man as a mirror one can predict good and bad luck." Have those who now regard offensive wars as beneficial made use of Chih Po's story ? It is plainly discernible to be not auspicious but ominous.

---

[1] This saying is found in the " Announcement about Drunkenness " in *Shu Ching*. Legge, vol. iii, part ii, p. 409.

CHAPTER XIX

CONDEMNATION OF OFFENSIVE WAR (III)

Motse said : What does the world now praise to be good ? Is not an act praised because it is useful to Heaven on high, to the spirits in the middle sphere, and to the people below ? Certainly no other reason is needed for praise than to be useful to Heaven on high, to the spirits in the middle, and to the people below. Even the stupid would say it is praiseworthy when it is helpful to Heaven on high, to the spirits in the middle, and to the people below. And what the world agrees on is just the way of the sage-kings.

Now the feudal lords in the empire still attack and assault each other. This is to praise the principle without understanding its real meaning. They resemble the blind man who uses with others the names of black and white but cannot discriminate between such objects. Can this be said to be real discrimination ?

Therefore, deliberating for the empire, the ancient wise men always considered the real (meaning of the) principles, and acted accordingly. Hence they were no more uncertain in their actions. All desires, far or near, were satisfied, and Heaven, the spirits, and the people were all blessed. Such was the way of the wise men. Governing the empire, the ancient magnanimous men always worked for mutual satisfaction with the large states, brought the empire into harmony, and centralized all that was within the four seas. Then they led the people in the empire diligently to do service to God, hills and rivers, and the spirits and ghosts. Many were the benefits to the people and great was their success. Thereupon Heaven rewarded them, the spirits enriched them, and the people praised them. The high honour of Son of Heaven was conferred upon them and the great wealth of the whole world was given to them. Their names partake of (the permanence and greatness of) Heaven and Earth and are not forgotten even to this day. Such is the way of the wise and such is the way by which the ancient kings came to possess the world.

The rulers and lords of to-day are quite different. They all rank their warriors and arrange their boat and chariot forces; they make their armour strong and weapons sharp in order to attack some innocent state. Entering the state they cut down the grain fields and fell the trees and woods; they tear down the inner and outer walls of the city and fill up the ditches and ponds; they seize and kill the sacrificial animals and burn down the ancestral temple; they kill and murder the people and exterminate the aged and weak; they move away the treasures and valuables. The soldiers are encouraged to advance by being told: " To suffer death is the highest (service you can render), to kill many is the next, to be wounded is the lowest. But if you should drop out from your rank and attempt to sneak away, the penalty will be death without moderation." Thus the soldiers are put to fear.

Now to capture a state and to destroy an army, to disturb and torture the people, and to set at naught the aspirations of the sages by confusion—is this intended to bless Heaven ? But the people of Heaven are gathered together to besiege the towns belonging to Heaven. This is to murder men of Heaven and dispossess the spirits of their altars and to ruin the state and to kill the sacrificial animals. It is then not a blessing to Heaven on high. Is it intended to bless the spirits ? But men of Heaven are murdered, spirits are deprived of their sacrifices, the earlier kings [1] are neglected, the multitude are tortured and the people are scattered ; it is then not a blessing to the spirits in the middle. Is it intended to bless the people ? But the blessing of the people by killing them off must be very meagre. And when we calculate the expense, which is the root of the calamities to living,[2] we find the property of innumerable people is exhausted. It is, then, not a blessing to the people below either.

Now that the armies are intended for mutual destruction, it is evident : If the general be not courageous, if soldiers be not brave, if weapons be not sharp, if drills be not frequent, if the force be not large, if generals be not harmonious, if power be not august, if a siege be not enduring, if an assault be not speedy, if people be not strongly bound together, if determination be not firm—if this be so, the (other) feudal lords will suspect. When feudal lords entertain suspicion, enemies will be stirred up and cause anxiety, and the morale will be weakened. On the other hand, if every preparation is in good shape and the state goes out to engage in war, then the state will lose its men and the people will neglect their vocations. Have we not heard it said that, when a warring state goes on an expedition, of the officers there

---

[1] Meaning the ancestral spirits of the state.

[2] This is an explicit expression of the common Chinese attitude towards the government as a mere tax-collecting agency.

must be several hundred, of the common people there must be several thousand, and of the soldiers and prisoners there must be ten thousand, before the army can set out ? It may last for several years, or, at the shortest, several months. So, the superior will have no time to attend to government, the officials will have no time to attend to their offices, the farmers will have no time to sow or reap, the women will have no time to weave or spin : that is, the state will lose its men and the people will neglect their vocations. Besides, the chariots will break and horses will be exhausted. As to tents, army supplies, and soldiers' equipment—if one-fifth of these can remain (after the war) it would already be beyond expectation. Moreover, innumerable men will be missing and lost on the way, and will become sick from the long distances, meagre rations, hunger and cold, and die in the ditches. Now the calamity to the people and the world is tremendous. Yet the rulers enjoy doing it. This means they enjoy injuring and exterminating the people ; is this not perversity ?

The most warring states in the empire to-day are Ch'i, Chin, Ch'u, and Yüeh. These four states are all successful in the world. Even if their people be increased tenfold, still they could not consume all that their land could produce. That is, they are in need of men while they have a surplus of land. Still they strove against each other to possess more land. This is to neglect what is needed and to value what is already in plenty.

The warring lords would gloss over (their conduct) with arguments to confute Motse, saying : " Do you condemn attack and assault as unrighteous and not beneficial ? But, anciently, Yü made war on the Prince of Miao, T'ang on Chieh, and King Wu on Chow. Yet these are regarded as sages. What is your explanation for this?" Motse said: You have not examined the terminology of my teaching and you do not understand its motive. What they did is not to be called "attack" 攻, but "punishment" 誅.

Anciently, the three Miao tribes were in great confusion. Heaven ordered their destruction. The sun rose at night. It rained blood for three days. Dragons emerged in the temple and dogs cried in the market place. Ice came in summer and earth cracked until water gushed forth. The five grains appeared in mutation. At these, the people were greatly shocked. Kao Yang [1] then gave command (to Yü) [1] in the Yuan Palace. Yü held the imperial jade order in hand and set forth to conquer Miao. Amidst thunder and lightning, a god with the face of a man and the body of a bird was revealed to be waiting upon (Yü) with the kuei [2] in hand. The general of Miao was brought down by an arrow,[3] and the Miao army was set in great confusion. And the Miao tribes became less and less significant ever after. Having conquered Miao, Yü set apart the hills and rivers (by names), and ordered things into high and low. With sacrifices he

---

[1] Kao Yang is an ancestor of Shun of the sixth generation. The insertion "(to Yü)" is made because this paragraph is intended to cite the circumstances under which Yü made war on the three Miao tribes. But if this is a story about Yü, then Kao Yang cannot appear in this connexion, as Yü is a later contemporary of Shun. The details of the whole story sound fictitious. More explanatory sentences seem to have been lost from the text.

[2] Kuei 珪 is a tablet of jade or ivory held by the minister when seeing the emperor.

[3] The text here contains two peculiar words, 搤 矢, whose meaning cannot be made out in this connexion. This seems to be a good guess.

set up the four bordering countries, and neither spirits nor men revolted (any more). So there was peace in the world. This was the reason why Yü made war on the Miao.

When it came to King Chieh of Hsia, Heaven gave severe order. Sun and moon did not appear on time. Winter and summer came irregularly. The five grains were dried up to death. Ghosts called in the country, and cranes shrieked for more than ten nights. Heaven then commissioned T'ang in the Piao Palace, to receive the great trust that had been given to Hsia, as the conduct of Hsia fell into great perversity. Only then dared T'ang to lead his multitude and enter the borders of Hsia. And he let the deserters of the enemy destroy the cities of Hsia. Soon after, a god came and told him : " The conduct of Hsia is in great confusion. Go and punish him. I will surely let you destroy him, as I have my orders from Heaven." Heaven ordered Chu Yung [1] to send down fire on the north-western corner of the city of Hsia. Thus T'ang led the men of Chieh and conquered Hsia. He then gave audience to the feudal lords at Po.[2] He revealed and made known the will of Heaven and spread it in the four directions, and none of the feudal lords in the empire dared to show disrespect. This was the reason why T'ang punished Chieh.

When it came to the regime of King Chow of Shang, his conduct was not acceptable to Heaven. Sacrifices were not according to seasons. Even in the night [3] . . . It rained sand for ten days at Po. The nine caldrons moved

---

[1] Chu Yung is the mythological god of fire, the Chinese Vulcan.
[2] Po then became the capital of Shang Dynasty.
[3] This sentence is incomplete in the text.

from their place. Witches appeared in the dark and ghosts
sighed at night. Some women turned into men. Flesh
came down from Heaven like rain. Thorny brambles covered
up the national highways. Yet the king became even more
dissolute. A red bird holding a kuei by its beak alighted
on Mt. Ch'i,[1] proclaiming : " Heaven decrees King Wen of
Chou to punish Yin [2] and possess its empire." T'ai Tien then
came to be minister to (King Wen). The charts emerged
out of the River and ch'eng-huang [3] appeared on land. Thereupon King Wu ascended the throne. Three gods spoke to
him in a dream, saying : " Now that we have submerged
Chow of Yin in wine, you go and attack him. We will surely
let you destroy him." So, King Wu set out and attacked
Chow, and replaced Shang with Chou. Heaven gave King
Wu the Yellow Bird Pennant. Having conquered Yin
he continued the order of T'ang and assigned the worship
of the ancestors of Chow to the feudal lords. Connexions
with the barbarians of the four borders were established,
and none in the world dared to show disrespect. This was
the reason why King Wu punished Chow.

Speaking about the work of these three sages, it is not
to be called attack but punishment.

The warring lords would again gloss over (their conduct)
with arguments for offensive war against Motse, saying :
" Do you condemn attack and assault as unrighteous and not

---

[1] Mount Ch'i is the geographical location of the state of Chou before it
overthrew Shang to become the succeeding dynasty in the Chinese Empire.

[2] Yin is the changed name of the Dynasty of Shang.

[3] Ch'eng-huang 乘 黃 is described as an animal of the family of fox.
Only, it has two horns on the back. This animal, if it ever existed, is now
extinct.

beneficial ?   But, in ancient times, Hsiung Li was assigned
to the state of Ch'u (about 1100 B.C.) in the Mt. of Sui.   Yi
K'uei started at Yu Chü, and became lord of Yüeh.   Uncle
T'ang and Lü Shang were first appointed to rule over the states
of Chin (1107 B.C.) and of Ch'i (about 1120 B.C.) respectively.   All these started with a few hundred li square of
land.   On account of their capture of other states, now each
of them has a quarter of the empire.   What is your explanation for this ? "

Motse said : You have not examined the terminology of my teachings and you do not understand the
underlying principle.   In ancient times the emperor commissioned feudal lords numbering more than ten thousand.
On account of absorption of one state by another, all of
the more than ten thousand states have disappeared with
only the four remaining.   This is like the physician who
attends more than ten thousand patients but cures only
four.   Such an one is not to be said to be a good
physician.

The warring lords would again gloss over (their conduct)
with arguments, saying : " (I wage war) not because I am
still discontented with my gold and jade, my children and
my land.   I want to have my name as a righteous ruler
established in the world and draw the other feudal lords to
me with my virtue."

Motse said : If there were some one who would
establish his righteous name for justice in the world
and draw the feudal lords to him with his virtue,
the submission of the whole world to him could be awaited
while standing.   For the world has long been in turmoil

and war, and it is weary like the boy at playing horse.[1] If only there were some one who would first benefit the other feudal lords in mutual good faith ! When some large state acts unrighteously, he would join in the sorrow ; when some large state attacks some smaller one he would join in the rescue ; when the outer and the inner walls of the city of the small state are in ruin he would demand their repair ; when cloth and grains are exhausted he would supply them ; when money and silk are insufficient he would share his own—to befriend the large state in this way, the large state will be pleased, to befriend the small state in this way, the small state will be pleased. With the others tired out and one's self at ease, one's armour and weapon [2] would be stronger. When with kindness and mercy we help the people in their need, the people will be drawn over. When good government is substituted for aggressive war, the country will be benefited many fold. When the expenses of the army is limited and the evils of the feudal lords removed, then we shall enjoy prosperity. Let the control (of the army) be judicious and the cause be righteous. Be lenient to the people and place confidence in the army—with this to meet the forces of the feudal lords, there can be no equal in the world. And the benefits to the world will be innumerable. This is what will benefit the world, yet the rulers do not understand making use of it : such may be said to be ignorance of the great thing in the world

---

[1] Meaning to tire one's self out for no benefit. *Infra*, p. 216.

[2] Armour and weapon here figuratively stand for resources of defence and offence.

Therefore Motse said : Now if the rulers and the gentlemen of the world sincerely desire to procure benefits and avert calamities for the world—if they desire to do righteousness and be superior men, if they desire to strike the way of the sage-kings on the one hand and bless the people on the other —if so, the doctrine of Condemnation of Offensive War should not be left unheeded.

BOOK VI

CHAPTER XX

ECONOMY OF EXPENDITURES (I)

When a sage rules a state the benefits of the state will be increased twice. When he governs the empire, those of the empire will be doubled. This increase is not by appropriating land from without. But by cutting out the useless expenditures it is accomplished. In issuing an order, taking up an enterprise, or employing the people and expending wealth, the sage never does anything without some useful purpose. Therefore wealth is not wasted and people's resources are not exhausted, and many are the blessings procured.

In making clothing, what is the purpose ? It is to keep out the cold in winter and heat in summer. The good of clothing is measured in terms of the amount of warmth it adds in winter and coolness in summer : what is merely decorative and does not contribute to these is to be let alone.

In building palaces and houses, what is the purpose ? It is to keep out the wind and the cold in winter and heat and rain in summer, and to fortify against thieves : what is merely decorative and contributes nothing to these should be let alone.

In forging armour and shields and the five weapons,[1] what is the purpose ? It is to prepare against invasions and revolts, bandits and thieves. When these happen, with

---

[1] The five weapons consist of sword, spear, etc. About the specific members making up the five weapons, commentators disagree. But the names of these are not translatable anyhow.

armour, shields, and the five weapons one will succeed, without
them one cannot succeed.   Therefore the sages forged armour,
shields, and the five weapons.   And their good is measured
in terms of lightness, sharpness and unbreakability : what
is merely decorative and contributes nothing to these should
be let alone.

In building boats and vehicles, what is the purpose ?
A vehicle is to go on land and a boat is to sail rivers and
valleys in order to transport the wealth in the four quarters.
The good of boats and vehicles is measured in terms of the
amount of facility and convenience they afford : what is
merely decorative and contributes nothing to these should
be let alone.

Now, in making all these things none is done without
its use in view.   Therefore wealth is not wasted and people's
resources are not exhausted, and many are the blessings
procured.

Besides, (the sages) again gave up all such hobbies as
collecting pearls and jade, and pet birds, and animals such
as dogs and horses, in order to replenish clothing, houses,
armour, shields, and the five weapons, and boats and vehicles.
And these were multiplied several times.   But to increase
these is not difficult.   What, then, is difficult to increase ?
To increase the population is difficult.

In ancient times, the sage-kings said : " No man of twenty
should dare to be without a family ; no girl of fifteen should
dare to be without a master."   Such were the laws of the
sage-kings.   Now that the sage-kings have passed away,
the people have become loose.   Those who like to have a
family early sometimes marry at twenty.   Those who like

to have a family late sometimes marry at forty.   When the late marriages are made up by the early ones, (the average) is still later than the legal requirements of the sage-kings by ten years.   Supposing births are given to children on an average of one in three years, then two or three children should have been born (by the time men now marry).   This is not just to urge men to establish families early in order to increase the population.   But also [1] . . . .

Those who govern the empire to-day diminish the people in more ways than one : Employing the people they exhaust them, levying taxes they make them heavy.   People fall into poverty and innumerable persons die of hunger and cold. Moreover the rulers make war and attack some neighbouring states.   It may last a whole year, or, at the shortest, several months.   Thus man and woman cannot see each other for a long time.   Is not this a way to diminish the people ? Living in danger, eating and drinking irregularly many become sick and die.   Hiding in ambush,[2] setting fire, besieging a city, and battling in the open fields, innumerable men die. Are not ways of diminishing the people getting numerous with the government of the rulers of to-day ?   They did not exist when the sage-kings administered the government. (In the government by the sagacious), many ways of increasing the population will arise.

Therefore Motse said : To cut out useless expenditures is the way of the sage-kings and a great blessing to the world.

---

[1] Text here incomplete.

[2] Text here not clear.   The rendition given above seems to be a good conjecture.

CHAPTER XXI

ECONOMY OF EXPENDITURES (II)

Motse said : The ancient illustrious kings and sages ruled over the empire and headed the feudal lords because they loved the people loyally and blessed them with many benefits. Loyalty calls out confidence. And, when blessing is shown in addition, the people were not wearied during their whole life and did not feel tired until their death. That the ancient illustrious kings and sages could rule over the empire and head the feudal lords is just because of this.

And the ancient sage-kings authorized the code of laws of economy, saying : " All you artisans and workers, carpenters and tanners, potters and smiths, do what you can do. Stop when the needs of the people are satisfied." What causes extra expense but adds no benefit to the people the sage-kings would not undertake.

The ancient sage-kings authorized the code of laws regarding food and drink, saying : " Stop when hunger is satiated, breathing becomes strong, limbs are strengthened and ears and eyes become sharp. There is no need of combining the five tastes [1] extremely well or harmonizing the different sweet odours. And efforts should not be made to procure rare delicacies from far countries." How do we know such were the laws ? In ancient times, when Yao was governing the empire he consolidated Chiao Tse [2] on the south, reached Yu Tu on the north, expanded from where the sun rises to

[1] The five tastes refer to Bitter, Hot, Sour, Sweet, and Salty.

[2] Chiao-Tse is the ancient name for what is now called West Indo-China.

where the sun sets on the east and west, and none was unsubmissive or disrespectful. Yet, even when he was served with what he much liked, he did not take a double cereal or both soup and meat. He ate out of an earthen liu 增 and drank out of an earthen hsing 形, and took wine out of a spoon. With the ceremonies of bowing and stretching and courtesies and decorum the sage-king had nothing to do.

The ancient sage-kings authorized the code of laws regarding clothing, saying : " Be satisfied with clothes of blue or grey silk in winter which are light and warm, and with clothes of flax-linen in summer which are light and cool." What causes extra expenditure but does not add benefits to the people the sage-kings would not allow.

Because the ferocious and cunning animals were destroying men and injuring the people, the ancient sage-kings taught the people the use of weapons, saying : " Carry a two-edged sword which penetrates when it pierces and severs when it cuts. When struck with the flat side it does not break, this is the utility of a sword. To be light and strong and afford convenience of action, such is the utility of an armour."

A vehicle is used to carry weight and to travel great distances. It should be safe to ride and easy to pull ; safe to ride so as not to hurt the rider, easy to pull so as to reach the destination speedily. This is the utility of the vehicle. Because the wide rivers and broad valleys were once not cross-able the sage-kings ordered boats and oars to be made. And these were made just so that they could cross the rivers. Even when the High Duke or a feudal lord arrived, the boat and the oars were not changed and the ferryman put on no decorations. Such is the utility of the boat.

The ancient sage-kings authorized the code of laws limiting funeral expenditure, saying : " Of shrouds. there shall be three pieces in order to be enough to hold the rotting flesh. The coffin shall be three inches thick, to be sufficient to hold the rotting bones. The pit shall be dug not deep enough to reach water, but just so deep that the gases will not escape. When the dead is buried the living shall not mourn too long."

In those ancient days, at the beginning of the race, when there were no palaces or houses, people lived in caves dug at the side of hills and mounds. The sage-kings felt quite concerned, thinking that the caves might keep off the wind and cold in winter, but that in summer it would be wet below and steaming above which might hurt the health of the people. So palaces and houses were built and found useful. Now, what is the standard in building palaces and houses ? Motse said : Just so that on the side it can keep off the wind and the cold, on top it can keep off the snow, frost, rain, and dew, within it is clean enough for sacrificial purposes, and that the partition in the palace is high enough to separate the men from the women. What causes extra expenditure but does not add any benefit to the people, the sage-kings will not undertake.

CHAPTER XXV

Simplicity in Funeral (III)

Motse said : The magnanimous ruler takes care of the empire, in the same way as a filial son takes care of his parents. But how does the filial son take care of his parents ? If the parents are poor he would enrich them ; if the parents have few people (descendants) he would increase them ; if the members (of the family) are in confusion he would put them in order. Of course, in doing this he might find his energy insufficient, his means limited, or his knowledge inadequate. But he dare not allow any energy, learning, or means unused to serve his parents. Such are the three interests of the filial son in taking care of his parents. And the same is true of the magnanimous ruler in taking care of the empire : if the empire is poor he would enrich it ; if the people are few he would increase them ; if the multitude are in confusion he would put them in order. Of course in doing these he might find his energy insufficient, means limited, or knowledge inadequate, but he dare not allow any energy, learning, or means unused to serve the world. And such are the three interests of the magnanimous ruler in taking care of the empire.

When the sage-kings of the Three Dynasties had passed away, and the world had become ignorant of their principles, some of the gentlemen in later generations regarded elaborate funeral and extended mourning as magnanimous, and righteous, and the duty of a filial son ; while others held them to be not magnanimous, not righteous, and not the duty of the

filial son. These two groups condemn each other in words
and contradict each other in deed, and yet both claim to be
followers of the way of Yao, Shun, Yü, T'ang, Wen, and Wu.
But since they are disagreed in word and opposed in deed,
people doubt the assertions of both. Now that the assertions
of both are doubted, it will be well to turn to the government
of the country and the people and see how elaborate funeral
and extended mourning affect the three interests. In my
opinion, if, in adopting the doctrine and practising the
principle, elaborate funeral and extended mourning could
enrich the poor, increase the few, remove danger, and regulate
disorder, it would be magnanimous, righteous, and the duty
of a filial son. Those who are to give counsel could not but
encourage it. And the magnanimous (ruler) would seek
to have it flourish in the empire and establish it so as to
have the people praise it and never disregard it in their
whole life. (On the other hand,) if, in adopting the
doctrine and practising the principle, elaborate funeral
and extended mourning really cannot enrich the poor,
increase the few, remove danger, and regulate disorder, it
will not be magnanimous, righteous, and the duty of the
filial son. Those who are to give counsel cannot but
discourage it. And the magnanimous will seek to have
it abolished in the empire and abandon it so as to have the
people condemn it, never to practise it in their whole life.
It has never happened, from ancient times to the present day,
that benefits are procured, calamities averted for the world,
and disorder among the people of the country is regulated
by elaborate funerals and extended mourning.

How do we know ?

For even at the present the gentlemen of the world are still doubtful whether elaborate funeral and extended mourning are right and beneficial.

Motse said : I have examined the sayings of those who uphold elaborate funeral and extended mourning. If they should be taken seriously in the country, it would mean [1] : when a lord dies, there would be several inner and outer coffins. He would be buried deep. There would be many shrouds. Embroidery would be elaborate. The grave mound would be massive. So, then, the death of a common man would exhaust the wealth of a family. And the death of a feudal lord would empty the state treasury before his body would be surrounded with gold, jade, and pearls, and the grave filled with carts and horses and bundles of silk. Further, there should be plenty of canopies and hangings, tings,[2] drums, tables, pots, and ice receptacles, spears, swords feather banners, and hides all to be carried along and buried. Not till then are the requirements considered fulfilled. And, regarding those who were to die to accompany their lord, for the emperor or a feudal lord there should be from several hundred to several tens, and for a minister or secretary there should be from several tens to several.

What are the rules to be observed by the mourner ? He must weep without restraint and sound as if he is choking. Sackcloth is worn on the breast and hat of flax on the head. His tears and snivel are not to be wiped away. The mourner is to live in a mourning hut, sleep on a coarse mat of straw,

---

[1] The following caricature is based on the Books of Ceremonial Records : Chou Li 周 禮, Yi Li 儀 禮, and Li Chi 禮 記.

[2] Ting 鼎 is a sacrificial vessel with three legs.

and lay his head on a lump of earth.   Then, he would be
obliged to abstain from food in order to look hungry, and to
wear little in order to look cold.   The face and eyes are to
look sunken and as if in fear, and the complexion is to appear
dark.   Ears and eyes are to become dull, and hands and feet
to become weak and unusable.   And, also, if the mourner
is a high official, he has to be supported to rise, and lean
on a cane to walk.   And all this is to last three years.

Adopting such a doctrine and practising such a principle :
rulers cannot come to court early [1] (and retire late ; the
officials cannot attend to the) five offices and six posts [2]
and encourage farming and forestry and fill the granaries ;
the farmers cannot start out early and come in late to cultivate
the land and plant trees ; the artisans cannot build boats
and vehicles and make vessels and utensils ; and the women
cannot rise early and retire late to weave and spin.   So,
then, in elaborate funerals much wealth is buried, and in
extended mourning abstention from work is prolonged.
Wealth already produced is carried away into the grave.
Child-bearing is postponed.   To seek wealth in this way
is like seeking a harvest by prohibiting farming.   The way
to wealth then is not here found.

Now that the practice of elaborate funerals and extended
mourning has failed to enrich the country perhaps it can
yet increase the population ?   Again it is powerless.   For
if elaborate funeral and extended mourning are adopted as

---

[1] The text here shows a break and is incomplete. The parenthesis inserted
seems to supply the loss.

[2] The five offices and six posts differ with different dynasties. At any rate,
they represent the several departments of the government.

the rule, then upon the death of the emperor there will be three years' mourning, upon the death of a parent there will be three years' mourning, upon the death of the wife or the eldest son there will be three years' mourning. There will be three years' mourning for all five (relations). Besides, there will be one year for uncles, brothers, and the other sons ; and five months for the near relatives, and also several months for aunts, sisters, nephews, and uncles on the mother's side. Further, there are set rules to emaciate one's health : the face and eyes are to look sunken and as if in fear, and the complexion is to appear dark. Ears and eyes are to become dull, and hands and feet are to become weak and unusable. And, also, if the mourner is a high official, he has to be supported to rise and lean on a cane to walk. And this is to last three years if such a doctrine is adopted and such a principle is practised. Being so hungry and weak, the people cannot stand the cold in winter and the heat in summer. And countless numbers will become sick and die. Sexual relations between husband and wife are prevented. To seek to increase the population by this way is like seeking longevity by thrusting one's self upon a sword. The way to dense population is not here found.

Now that it has failed to increase the population, perhaps it can yet regulate jurisdiction ? Again it is powerless. For, adopting elaborate funerals and extended mourning as a principle in government, the state will become poor, the people few, and the jurisdiction disorderly. Adopting such a doctrine and practising such a principle superiors cannot give attention to administration and subordinates cannot attend to their work. When the superiors are unable to give their attention to administration there will be disorder.

When the subordinates are unable to attend to their work, the supply of food and clothing will be insufficient. When there is insufficiency, the undutiful younger brother will ask his older brother for help, and when he does not receive it he will hate the elder brother. The unfilial son will turn to his father for help and when he does not receive it he will spurn his father. And the disloyal minister will turn for help to his lord and when he does not receive it he will mock his lord. And vicious and immoral people will commit evil and immorality beyond control when they are without clothing abroad and without food at home. So, bandits and thieves will be numerous but law-abiding people few. Now, to seek order by multiplying the bandits and thieves and diminishing the law-abiding people is like demanding of a person not to present his back to you after making him turn around three times. The way to order is not here found.

Now that it has failed to regulate jurisdiction and government, perhaps it can yet prevent the large states from attacking the small states ? Again it is powerless. For since the ancient sage-kings have passed away and the world has become ignorant of their principles, the feudal lords resort to attack by force. On the south there are the kings of Ch'u and Yüeh, and on the north there are the lords of Ch'i and Chin. All of these show favours and encouragement to their warriors and soldiers, making it their business in the world to attack and absorb (others). Some small states, however, they do not attack, and this because these small states are well stored with supplies, their inner and outer city walls are in repair, and in them the superior and the subordinates are harmonious. Therefore the large states would not want to attack them. Those which are not well stored with supplies, whose inner and outer city walls are not in repair, and in which the superior and the subordinates are not harmonious, the large states would want to attack. Adopting elaborate funerals and extended mourning in government, the state will become poor, the people few, and jurisdiction disorderly. Since the state is poor, no surplus goods can be stored. Since its numbers are few, there will be few workmen to keep the city walls and moats in repair. Since it is disorderly, a state will not be victorious in attack or strong in defence.

Now that it has failed in preventing the large states from attacking the small states, perhaps it can yet procure blessing from God and the spirits. Again it is powerless. For, adopting elaborate funeral and extended mourning as a principle in government, the state will become poor, the people few, and the jurisdiction disorderly. When the state is poor the cakes and wine will be unclean. When the people are few the worshippers of God and the spirits will be reduced in number. And when jurisdiction is in disorder the sacrifice will not be made according to season. Moreover, the worship of God and the spirits is now even prohibited. When the government is run like this, God and the spirits would deliberate from on high, saying : " Which is better, to have these people exist or not to have them exist ? It really makes no difference whether they exist or not." Therefore God and spirits will send judgment upon them and visit them with calamities and punish and desert them. Is not this quite in place ?

Therefore the ancient sage-kings[1] authorized the code of laws regarding the burial of the dead thus : The coffin shall be three inches thick, sufficient to hold the body. As to shrouds there shall be three pieces adequate to cover the corpse. It shall not be buried so deep as to reach water and neither so shallow as to allow the odour to ascend. Three feet in size shall be big enough for the mound. There shall be no extended mourning after burial, but speedy return to work and pursuit in what one can do to procure mutual benefit. Such are the laws of the sage-kings.

Those who uphold elaborate funerals and extended mourning say : " Although elaborate funerals and extended mourning cannot enrich the poor, increase the few, remove danger and regulate disorder, yet they were a principle of the sage-kings."

Motse replied : Not at all. Anciently, Yao went north to instruct the eight tribes of Ti.[2] He died on the way and was buried in the shade [3] of Mt. Ch'iung. Of shrouds there were three pieces. The coffin was of soft wood, and sealed with flax linen. Weeping started only after burial. There was no mound, only the pit was filled up. After burial, oxen and horses plodded over it. Shun went west to instruct the seven tribes of Jung.[2] He died on the way and was buried in the market place of Nan Chi. Of shrouds there were three pieces. The coffin was of soft wood and sealed with flax linen. After burial the people in the market place walked over it. Yü went east to instruct the nine tribes of Yi.[2] He died on the way and was buried at Mt. Kuei Chi.

[1] Here Motse mainly refers to Yü, who of all the sage-kings advocates the simplest ceremonies.
[2] Names of different aboriginal tribes surrounding China then.
[3] Meaning south of Mount Ch'iung.

Of clothing there were three pieces. The coffin was of t'ung wood [1] and sealed with flax linen. It did not crush when bound, and it did not sink in when pressed. The pit was not deep enough to strike water and not so shallow as to allow the odour to ascend. When the coffin had been buried, the remaining earth was gathered on it, and the mound was three feet high and no more. So, to judge according to these three sage-kings, elaborate funerals and extended mourning were really not the way of the sage-kings. These three sage-kings held the rank of Sons of Heaven and possessed the whole empire, yet they authorized their burial in this way; was it because of any fear of lack of means ?

The way in which the present rulers are buried is quite different from this. There are the outer and the inner coffins, and then the three layers of hide and embroidered covers. When the stones and jade are all collected, there are yet to be completed the spears, swords, tings, pots and ice receptacles, and ten thousand of decorated reins and yokes, and the carriages, horses, and the chorus girls. Then, there must be built the tunnel to reach under the tomb which is as high as a hill. This interferes with people's work and wastes people's wealth to such a great extent. How indeed is this to be avoided ?

So Motse said : I have already said that if, in adopting the doctrine and practising the principle, elaborate funeral and extended mourning really could enrich the poor, increase the few, remove danger and regulate disorder, they would be magnanimous, righteous, and the duty of the filial son.

---

[1] T'ung 桐 is a large tree belonging to the Euphorbiaceæ or *Elæococca sinensis.*

Those who give counsel could not but encourage them.
(On the other hand,) if, in adopting the doctrine and practising
the principle, elaborate funeral and extended mourning
really cannot enrich the poor, increase the few, remove danger
and regulate disorder, they are not magnanimous, righteous,
and the duty of the filial son. Those who are to give counsel
cannot but discourage it. Now, (we have seen) that to seek
to enrich a country thereby brings about poverty ; to seek
to increase the people thereby results in a decrease ; and to
seek to regulate government thereby begets disorder. To
seek to prevent the large states from attacking the small
ones by this way is impossible on the one hand, and, on the
other, to seek to procure blessing from God and the spirits
through it only brings calamity. When we look up and
examine the ways of Yao, Shun, Yü, T'ang, Wen, and Wu,
we find it is diametrically opposed to (these). But when
we look down and examine the regimes of Chieh, Chow,
Yu, and Li, we find it agrees with these like two parts of
a tally. So, judging from these, elaborate funeral and
extended mourning are not the way of the sage-kings.

Those who uphold elaborate funeral and extended mourning
are saying : " If the elaborate funerals and extended mourning
were not the way of the sage-kings, why then do the gentlemen
of the Middle Kingdom [1] practise them continually and follow
them without discrimination ? "

Motse said : This is because habit affords convenience
and custom carries approval. Anciently, east of the state

[1] " Middle Kingdom " 中 國 was used by the Chinese themselves to refer
to the Chinese Empire in contrast to the surrounding barbarian tribes, and
semi-barbarian states like Ch'u and Yüeh.

of Yüeh there was the tribe of K'ai Shu. Among them the first-born son was dismembered and devoured after birth and this was said to be propitious for his younger brothers. When the father died the mother was carried away and abandoned, and the reason was that one should not live with the wife of a ghost. By the officials this was regarded as a government regulation and by the people it was accepted as a commonplace. They practised it continually and followed it without discrimination. Was it then the good and the right way ? No, this is really because habit affords convenience and custom carries approval. South of Ch'u there was a cannibal tribe.[1] Upon the death of the parents the flesh was scraped off and thrown away, while the bones were buried. And by following this custom one became a filial son. West of the state of Ch'in there was the tribe of Yi Ch'ü. Upon their death the parents were burned on a bonfire and amidst the smoke, and this was said to be ascension to the golden clouds. In this way one became a filial son. The officials embodied it in the government regulations and the people regarded it as a commonplace. They practised it continually and followed it without discrimination. Is it then the good and the right way ? No, this is really because habit affords convenience and custom carries approval.

Now, the practice of these three tribes is too heartless and that of the gentlemen of the Middle Kingdom is too elaborate. This being too elaborate and that being to heartless, then there should be rules for funerals and burials. Even regarding clothing and food, which are the necessities

---

[1] There is a more detailed description of the practice of this tribe on p. 246f.

of life, there are rules.   How then can there be none regarding
funerals and burials, which are the necessities of death ?
Outlining the rules for funerals and burials, Motse said :
The coffin shall be three inches thick, just sufficient to hold
the rotting bones.   Of shrouds there shall be three pieces
just to be enough to hold the rotting flesh.   The pit shall
be dug not so deep as to strike water, and not so shallow
as to allow the odour to ascend.   The mound shall be just
high enough to be identified (by the mourners).   There may
be weeping on the way to and from the burial.   But upon
returning they shall engage in earning the means of livelihood.
Sacrifices shall not be neglected in order to express one's
filial piety to parents.   Thus the rules of Motse neglect the
necessities of neither the dead nor the living.

Hence, Motse said : If the gentlemen of the world really
want to practise righteousness and magnanimity, and to
seek to be superior men, desiring to attain the way of the
sage-kings on the one hand and to procure blessings for the
people on the other, they cannot afford to neglect the principle
of Simplicity in Funeral in government.

BOOK VII

CHAPTER XXVI

Will of Heaven (I)

Motse said: The gentlemen of the world all understand only trifles but not things of importance. How do we know? We know this from one's conduct in the family. If one should offend the patriarch of the family, there are still the homes of the neighbours in which to seek shelter. Yet parents, brothers, and friends all keep on reminding one to be obedient and careful. For, how can one offend the patriarch and stay in the family? Not only is this true about conduct in the family, but also in the state. If one should offend the lord of the state there are still the neighbouring states whither he may flee. Yet parents, brothers, and friends all keep on reminding one to be obedient and careful. For, how can one offend the lord of the state and stay in it? From these there are yet shelters to flee to, yet there are such constant counsels. Should there not be more counsels in a case from which there is nowhere to flee? As the saying goes: " Sinning in broad daylight, whither can one flee? " Really there is nowhere to flee. For, Heaven clearly discerns it even if it be in the woods, valleys, or solitary caves where there is no man. But, contrary to our expectation, regarding Heaven, the gentlemen of the world do not understand mutually to give counsel. This is how we know the gentlemen in the world understand only trifles and not things of importance.

Now, what does Heaven desire and what does it abominate ? Heaven desires righteousness and abominates unrighteousness. Therefore, in leading the people in the world to engage in doing righteousness I should be doing what Heaven desires. When I do what Heaven desires, Heaven will also do what I desire. Now, what do I desire and what do I abominate ? I desire blessings and emoluments, and abominate calamities and misfortunes. When I do not do what Heaven desires, neither will Heaven do what I desire. Then I should be leading the people into calamities and misfortunes. But how do we know Heaven desires righteousness and abominates unrighteousness ? For, with righteousness the world lives and without it the world dies ; with it the world becomes rich and without it the world becomes poor ; with it the world becomes orderly and without it the world becomes chaotic. And Heaven likes to have the world live and dislikes to have it die,[1] likes to have it rich and dislikes to have it poor, and likes to have it orderly and dislikes to have it disorderly. Therefore we know Heaven desires righteousness and abominates unrighteousness.

Moreover, righteousness is the standard. A standard is not to be given by the subordinates to the superior but by the superior to the subordinates. Therefore, while the common people should spare no pains at work they may not make the standard at will. There are the scholars to give them the standard. While the scholars should spare no pains at work, they may not make the standard at will. There are the ministers and secretaries to give them the standard.

---

[1] This idea may be taken as the Chinese and humanistic counterpart of the Western classical assumption that being is better than non-being.

While the ministers and secretaries should spare no pains at work, they may not make the standard at will. There are the high duke and feudal lords to give them the standard. While the high duke and the feudal lords should spare no pains at work, they may not make the standard at will. There is the emperor to give them the standard. The emperor may not make the standard at will (either). There is Heaven to give him the standard. That the emperor gives the standard to the high duke, to the feudal lords, to the scholars, and to the common people, the gentlemen in the world clearly understand. But that Heaven gives the standard to the emperor, the people do not know well. Therefore the ancient sage-kings of the Three Dynasties, Yü, T'ang, Wen, and Wu, desiring to make it clear to the people that Heaven gives the standard to the emperor, fed oxen and sheep with grass, and pigs and dogs with grain, and cleanly prepared the cakes and wine to do sacrifice to God on High and the spirits, and invoked Heaven's blessing. But I have not yet heard of Heaven invoking the emperor for blessing. So I know Heaven gives the standard to the emperor.

The emperor is the most honourable of the world and the richest of the world. So, the honoured and the rich cannot but obey the will of Heaven. He who obeys the will of Heaven, loving universally and benefiting others, will obtain rewards. He who opposes the will of Heaven, by being partial and unfriendly and harming others, will incur punishment. Now, who were those that obeyed the will of Heaven and obtained rewards, and who were those that opposed the will of Heaven and incurred punishment ?

Motse said : The ancient sage-kings of the Three Dynasties,

Yü, T'ang, Wen, and Wu, were those that obeyed the will
of Heaven and obtained reward. And the wicked kings
of the Three Dynasties, Chieh, Chow, Yu, and Li, were those
that opposed the will of Heaven and incurred punishment.
How did Yü, T'ang, Wen, and Wu obtain their reward ?

Motse said : In the highest sphere they revered Heaven,
in the middle sphere they worshipped the spirits, and in the
lower sphere they loved the people. Thereupon the will of
Heaven proclaimed : " All those whom I love these love also,
and all those whom I benefit these benefit also. Their love
to men is all-embracing and their benefit to men is most
substantial." And so, they were raised to the honour of
Sons of Heaven and enriched with the heritage of the empire.
They were succeeded by descendants for ten thousand [1]
generations to continue the spread of their righteousness
all over the world. And people praise them unto this day,
calling them righteous sage-kings.

How did Chieh, Chow, Yu, and Li incur their punishment ?

Motse said : In the highest sphere they blasphemed against
Heaven, in the middle sphere they blasphemed against
the spirits, and in the sphere below they oppressed the people.
Thereupon the will of Heaven proclaimed : " From those
whom I love these turn away and hate, and those whom
I want to benefit they oppress. Their hate of men is without
limit and their oppression of men the most severe." And,
so, they were not permitted to finish out their lives,[2] or to
survive a single generation. And people condemn them
unto this day, calling them wicked kings.

[1] A common Chinese figure for many.
[2] Meaning to die unnaturally.

How do we know Heaven loves the people ? Because it teaches them all. How do we know it teaches them all ? Because it claims them all. How do we know it claims them all ? Because it accepts sacrifices from them all. How do we know it accepts sacrifices from all ? Because within the four seas all who live on grains [1] feed oxen and sheep with grass, and dogs and pigs with grains, and prepare clean cakes and wine to do sacrifice to God on High and the spirits. Claiming all the people, why will Heaven not love them ? Moreover, as I have said, for the murder of one innocent individual there will be one calamity. Who is it that murders the innocent ? It is man. Who is it that sends down the calamity ? It is Heaven. If Heaven should be thought of as not loving the people, why should it send down calamities for the murder of man by man ? So, I know Heaven loves the people.

To obey the will of Heaven is to accept righteousness as the standard. To oppose the will of Heaven is to accept force as the standard. Now what will the standard of righteousness do ?

Motse said : He who rules a large state does not attack small states : he who rules a large house does not molest small houses. The strong does not plunder the weak. The honoured does not disdain the humble. The clever does not deceive the stupid. This is beneficial to Heaven above, beneficial to the spirits in the middle sphere, and beneficial to the people below. Being beneficial to these three it is beneficial to all. So the most excellent name is attributed to such a man and he is called sage-king.

[1] Mark of civilization of the agricultural stage.

The standard of force is different from this. It is contradictory to this in word and opposed to this in deed like galloping with back to back. Leading a large state, he whose standard is force attacks small states ; leading a large house he molests small houses. The strong plunders the weak. The honoured disdains the humble. The clever deceives the stupid. This is not beneficial to Heaven above, or to the spirits in the middle sphere, or to the people below. Not being beneficial to these three, it is beneficial to none. So, the most evil name in the world is attributed to him and he is called the wicked king.

Motse said : The will of Heaven to me is like the compasses to the wheelwright and the square to the carpenter. The wheelwright and the carpenter measure all the square and circular objects with their square and compasses and accept those that fit as correct and reject those that do not fit as incorrect. The writings of the gentlemen of the world of the present day cannot be all loaded (in a cart), and their doctrines cannot be exhaustively enumerated. They endeavour to convince the feudal lords on the one hand and the scholars on the other. But from magnanimity and righteousness they are far off. How do we know ? Because I have the most competent standard in the world to measure them with.

CHAPTER XXVII

WILL OF HEAVEN (II)

Motse said : Those gentlemen in the world who want to practise magnanimity and righteousness cannot but examine the origin of righteousness. Since we want to examine the origin of righteousness, then where does it originate ?

Motse said : Righteousness does not originate with the stupid and humble but with the honourable and wise. How do we know it does not originate with the dull and humble but with the honourable and wise ? For, righteousness is the standard. How do we know righteousness is the standard ? For, with righteousness the world will be orderly and without it the world will be disorderly. Therefore righteousness is known to be the standard. As the dull and the humble cannot make the standard, and only the wise and honourable can, therefore I know righteousness does not come from the stupid and humble but from the honourable and wise.

Now who is honourable and who is wise ? Heaven is honourable, Heaven is wise. So, then, righteousness must originate with Heaven. People in the world would say : " That the emperor is more honourable than the feudal lords and that the feudal lords are more honourable than the ministers, we clearly see. But that Heaven is more honourable and wise than the emperor, we do not see."

Motse said : I know Heaven is more honourable and wise than the emperor for a reason : When the emperor practises virtue Heaven rewards, when the emperor does evil Heaven punishes. When there are disease and calamities the emperor will purify and bathe himself and prepare clean cakes and wine to do sacrifice and libation to Heaven and the spirits. Heaven then removes them. But I have not yet heard of Heaven invoking the emperor for blessing. So I know Heaven is more honourable and wise than the emperor. And, this is not all. We also learn of this from the book of the ancient kings which instructs us the vast and ineffable Tao of Heaven. It says: " Brilliant and perspicacious Heaven on High, who enlightens and watches over the earth below ! " [1] This shows Heaven is more honourable and wise than the emperor. But is there yet any one more honourable and wise than Heaven ? Heaven is really the most honourable and wise. Therefore, righteousness surely comes from Heaven. And hence Motse said : If the gentlemen of the world really desire to follow the way and benefit the people, they must not disobey the will of Heaven, the origin of magnanimity and righteousness.

Now that we must obey the will of Heaven, what does the will of Heaven desire and what does it abominate ? Motse said : The will of Heaven abominates the large state which attacks small states, the large house which molests small houses, the strong who plunder the weak, the clever who deceive the stupid, and the honoured who disdain the humble—these are what the will of Heaven abominates. On the other hand, it desires people having energy to work for each other, those knowing the way to teach each other,

---

[1] These are the two opening lines of the ode " Hsiao Ming " in *Shih Ching.* Legge, vol. iv, p. 363, renders it thus :—

" O bright and high Heaven,
Who enlightenest and rulest this lower world ! '

and those possessing wealth to share with each other. And it desires the superior diligently to attend to government and the subordinates diligently to attend to their work. When the superior attends to the government diligently, the country will be orderly. When the subordinates attend to work diligently, wealth will be abundant. When the country is orderly and wealth is abundant, within the state there will be wherewith to prepare clean cakes and wine to sacrifice to God and the spirits, and in relation with outside countries there will be wherewith to furnish rings, stones, pearls, and jades by which to befriend surrounding neighbours. With the grudges of the feudal lords inactive and fighting on the borders suspended, and the people within provided with food and rest, the emperor and the ministers and the superiors and subordinates will be gracious and loyal respectively, and father and son and elder and younger brothers will be affectionate and filial respectively. Therefore when the principle of obeying the will of Heaven is understood and widely practised in the world, then justice and government will be orderly, the multitudes will be harmonious, the country will be wealthy, the supplies will be plenteous, and the people will be warmly clothed and sufficiently fed, peaceful and without worry. Therefore Motse said : If the gentlemen of the world really desire to follow the way and benefit the people they must carefully investigate the principle that the will of Heaven is the origin of magnanimity and righteousness.

The rule of Heaven over the world is not unlike the rule of the feudal lord over the state. In ruling the state does the feudal lord desire his ministers and people to work for mutual disadvantage ? If leading a large state one attacks small states, if leading a large house one molests small houses —if by doing this one seeks reward and commendation (from the feudal lord) he cannot obtain it. On the contrary, punishment will visit him. Now, the rule of Heaven over the world is not unlike this. If leading a large state one attacks small states, if leading a large house one molests small houses—if by doing this one seeks reward and commendation (from Heaven) he cannot obtain it. On the contrary, punishment will visit him. When (man) does not do what Heaven desires, but does what Heaven abominates, Heaven will also not do what man desires but do what he abominates. What man abominates are disease and calamities. Therefore not to do what Heaven desires but do what it abominates is to lead the multitudes in the world to calamity. Therefore the ancient sage-kings studied what Heaven and the spirits would bless and avoided what they would curse in order to procure benefits for the world and avoid calamities. Thereupon, Heaven made heat and cold temperate, the four seasons harmonious, the Yin and Yang and rain and dew timely. The five grains are enabled to ripen and the six animals to mature. And disease, pestilence, and famine did not happen. Therefore Motse said : If the gentlemen of the world really desire to follow the Tao and benefit the people they must be mindful of the principle that the will of Heaven is the origin of magnanimity and righteousness.

In the world those who lack benevolence are unfortunate. If a son does not serve his father, a younger brother does not serve his elder brother, or a subordinate does not serve his superior, then all the gentlemen of the world will call him unfortunate. Now Heaven loves the whole world universally. Everything is prepared [1] for the good of man. Even the tip of a hair is the work of Heaven. Substantial may be said of the benefits that are enjoyed by man. Yet there is no service in return. And they do not even know this to be unmagnanimous and unfortunate. This is why I say the gentlemen understand only trifles and not things of importance.

Moreover I know Heaven loves men dearly not without reason. Heaven ordered the sun, the moon, and the stars to enlighten and guide them. Heaven ordained the four seasons, Spring, Autumn, Winter, and Summer, to regulate them. Heaven sent down snow, frost, rain, and dew to grow the five grains and flax and silk [2] that so the people could use and enjoy them. Heaven established the hills and rivers, ravines and valleys, and arranged many things to minister to man's good or bring him evil. He appointed the dukes and lords to reward the virtuous and punish the wicked, and to gather metal and wood, birds and beasts, and to engage in cultivating the five grains and flax and silk to provide for the people's food and clothing. This has been taking place from antiquity to the present. Suppose there is a man who is deeply fond of his son and has used his energy to the limit to work for his benefit. But when the son grows up he returns no love to the father. The gentlemen of the world will all call him unmagnanimous and miserable. Now Heaven

---

[1] The term here used in the text is "chiao sui" 撽 逐. Its exact meaning is not ascertainable.

[2] Meaning mulberry.

loves the whole world universally. Everything is prepared [1]
for the good of man. The work of Heaven extends to even
the smallest things that are enjoyed by man. Such benefits
may indeed be said to be substantial, yet there is no service
in return. And they do not even know this to be unmagnanimous. This is why I say the gentlemen of the world
understand only trifles but not things of importance.[2]

Yet this does not exhaust my reasons whereby I know
Heaven loves man dearly. It is said the murder of an innocent
individual will call down a calamity. Who is the innocent ?
Man is. From whom is the visitation ? From Heaven.
If Heaven does not love the people dearly, why should Heaven
send down a visitation upon the man who murders the
innocent ? Thus I know Heaven loves man dearly.

This is still not all by which I know Heaven loves man
dearly. There are those who love the people and benefit
the people and obey the will of Heaven and obtain reward
from Heaven. There are also those who hate the people
and oppress the people and oppose the will of Heaven and
incur punishment from Heaven. Who are those that love

---

[1] *Supra*, p. 145, note 1.

[2] Compare this theme of Motse's with the following from Seneca, *On
Benefits*, iv, 6 : " We can be thankful to a friend for a few acres, or a little
money ; and yet for the freedom and command of the whole earth, and for
the great benefits of our being, as life, health, and reason, we look upon
ourselves as under no obligation. If a man bestows upon us a house that is
delicately beautified with painting, statues, gildings, and marbles, we
make a mighty business of it, and yet it lies at the mercy of a puff of wind,
the snuff of a candle, and a hundred other accidents to lay it in the dust.
And is it nothing now to sleep under the canopy of heaven, where we have
the globe of the earth as our place of repose, and the glories of the heavens
for our spectacle ? "

the people and benefit the people, obey the will of Heaven
and obtain reward from Heaven ? They are the ancient
sage-kings of the Three Dynasties, Yao, Shun, Yü, T'ang,
Wen, and Wu. What did Yao, Shun, Yü, T'ang, Wen,
and Wu do ? They engaged themselves in universality
and not partiality (in love). Loving universally, they did
not attack the small states with their large states, they did
not molest the small houses with their large houses. The
strong did not plunder the weak, the many did not
oppress the few, the clever did not deceive the stupid, the
honoured did not disdain the humble. Such a regime was
agreeable to Heaven above, to the spirits in the middle sphere,
and to the people below. Being helpful to these three,
it was helpful to all. And this was Heavenly virtue. The
most excellent names in the world were gathered and
attributed to them, and they were called magnanimous,
righteous, beloved of man and beneficial to the people,
obedient to the will of Heaven and rewarded of Heaven.

Besides this, it is also recorded on the bamboos and silk,
cut in metals and stones, and engraved on the dishes and
cups to be handed down to posterity. What is this for ?
It is to mark out those who loved the people and benefited
them, obeyed the will of Heaven and obtained reward from
Heaven. Thus the ode of Huang Yi says : " God said to King
Wen, ' I cherish your intelligent virtue. It was not proclaimed
with much noise or gesture. It was not modified after the
possession of the empire. How instructively and naturally
submissive to the scheme of Heaven ! ' " [1] Because he was

---

[1] This is the seventh stanza of the ode of " Huang Yi" in *Shih Ching*.
It is a narration of the rise of the dynasty of Chou and the deeds of

obedient to God's scheme, He rewarded him with Yin [1] and honoured him to be emperor and enriched him with the empire. And his fame is not forgotten even unto this day. Hence we are enabled to know who are those that loved the people and benefited them, obeyed the will of Heaven and obtained reward from Heaven.

Now, who are those that hated the people and oppressed them, opposed the will of Heaven and incurred punishment from Heaven ? They are the ancient wicked kings of the Three Dynasties, Chieh, Chow, Yu, and Li. What did they do ? They were selfish and ungenerous. Being selfish they attacked the small states with their large states, they molested the small houses with their large houses. The strong plundered the weak, the many oppressed the few, the clever deceived the ignorant, the honoured disdained the humble. Such a regime was not helpful to Heaven above, to the spirits in the middle sphere, or to the people below. Since it was not helpful to these three it was helpful to none. And they were called the enemies of Heaven. The most evil names in the world were gathered and attributed to them, and they were called unmagnanimous, unrighteous, haters of man and oppressors of the people, disobedient to the will of Heaven and punished by Heaven. Besides this,

---

some of its early kings. According to Legge, vol. iv, p. 454, the stanza reads : " God said to King Wan :—

　　　' I am pleased with your intelligent virtue,
　　　Not loudly proclaimed nor portrayed,
　　　Without extravagance or changeableness,
　　　Without consciousness of effort on your part,
　　　In accordance with the pattern of God.' "

[1] I.e. God gave him the succession to the dynasty of Yin.

it is also recorded on the bamboos and silk, cut in the metals
and stones, and engraved on the plates and cups to be handed
down to posterity.   What is this for ?   It is to mark out
those that hated the people and oppressed them, opposed
the will of Heaven and incurred punishment from Heaven.
Thus relates the " Great Declaration " : " Chow went beyond
the proper limits and became insolent.   He would not worship
God and pushed away the ancestors and spirits without
offering them sacrifices.   And he said : ' Fortune is with me,'
and neglected and betrayed his duty.   Heaven thereupon
deserted him and withdrew its protection." [1]   Heaven
deserted Chow and withdrew its support because Chow
opposed the will of Heaven.   Hence we are enabled to know
who are those that hated the people and oppressed them,
opposed the will of Heaven and incurred punishment from
Heaven.

Therefore the will of Heaven is like the compasses to the
wheelwright and the square to the carpenter. The wheelwright tests the circularity of every object in the world
with his compasses, saying :   " That which satisfies my
compasses is circular.   That which does not is not circular."
Therefore whether an object is circular or not is all known,
because the standard of circularity is all established.   The
carpenter also tests the squareness of every object in the

---

[1] The text we now have of the " Great Declaration " in *Shu Ching* is quite
different. For comparison Legge is here quoted, vol. iii, pp. 285–6 : " But
Show has no repentent heart. He abides squatting on his heels, not serving
God or the spirits of Heaven and Earth, neglecting also the temple of his
ancestors, and not sacrificing in it. The victims and the vessels of millet
all become the prey of wicked robbers ; and still he says, ' The people are
mine : The decree is mine,' never trying to correct his contemptuous mind."

world with his square, saying : " That which satisfies my square is square ; that which does not is not square." Therefore whether any object is square or not is all known. Why so ? Because the standard of squareness is established. Similarly, with the will of Heaven Motse will measure the jurisdiction and government of the lords in the empire on the one hand, and the doctrines and teachings of the multitudes in the empire on the other. If some conduct is observed to be in accordance with the will of Heaven, it is called good conduct ; if it is in opposition to the will of Heaven it is called bad conduct. If a teaching is observed to be in accordance with the will of Heaven it is called good teaching ; if it is in opposition to the will of Heaven it is called bad teaching. And if a government is observed to be in accordance with the will of Heaven it is called good government ; if it is in opposition to the will of Heaven it is called bad government. With this as the model and with this as the standard, whether the lords and the ministers are magnanimous or not can be measured as (easily as) to distinguish black and white. Therefore Motse said : If the rulers and the gentlemen of the world really desire to follow the way and benefit the people they have only to obey the will of Heaven, the origin of magnanimity and righteousness. Obedience to the will of Heaven is the standard of righteousness.

CHAPTER XXVIII

WILL OF HEAVEN (III)

Motse said : What is the reason for the disorder in the world ? It is because the gentlemen of the world all understand trifles but not things of importance. How do we know they understand trifles but not things of importance ? Because they do not understand the will of Heaven. How do we know they do not understand the will of Heaven ? By observing the conduct in the family. If a man commits a misdemeanour in the family he still has other families in which to seek shelter. Yet, father reminds son, the elder brother reminds the younger brother, saying : " Be obedient, be careful in conduct in the family. If one is not obedient and careful in conduct in the family how can he live in the state ? " If a man commits a misdemeanour in the state he still has other states in which to seek shelter. Yet father reminds son and the elder brother reminds the younger brother, saying : " Be obedient. Be careful. One cannot live in a state and be disobedient and careless." Now all men live in the world and under Heaven. When a man sins against Heaven there is nowhere to seek shelter. But people do not think of warning each other. Thus I know that they do not understand things of importance. And Motse said : Be obedient. Be careful. Be sure to do what Heaven desires and avoid what Heaven abominates.

Now, what does Heaven desire and what does Heaven abominate ? Heaven desires righteousness and abominates

unrighteousness.   How do we know this ?   Because righteousness is the standard.   How do we know righteousness is the
standard ?   Because with righteousness the world will be
orderly ; without it the world will be disorderly.   So, I know
righteousness is the standard.   Now a standard is never given
by the subordinate to the superior, it is always to be given by
the superior to the subordinate.   Hence the common people
may not make the standard at will.   There are the scholars
to give them the standard.   The scholars may not make the
standard at will.   There are the ministers to give them the
standard.   The ministers may not make the standard at
will.   There are the feudal lords to give them the standard.
The feudal lords may not make the standard at will.   There
is the high duke to give them the standard.   The high duke
may not make the standard at will.   There is the emperor
to give him the standard.   The emperor may not make the
standard at will.   There is Heaven to give him the standard.
The gentlemen of the world all understand that the emperor
gives the standard to the world but do not understand that
Heaven gives the standard to the emperor.   The sages,
explaining this, said : " When the emperor has done good,
Heaven rewards him.   When the emperor has committed
wrong, Heaven punishes him.   When the emperor is unjust
in reward and punishment and not judicious in hearing
lawsuits, Heaven visits him with disease and calamities,
and frost and dew will be untimely." The emperor will
then have to feed oxen and sheep with grass and dogs
and pigs with grains and prepare clean cakes and wine to
pray and invoke Heaven for blessing.   I have not yet
heard of Heaven praying and invoking the emperor for

blessing. So, I can say Heaven is more honourable and wise than the emperor. Therefore righteousness does not come from the ignorant and humble but from the honourable and wise. Who is honourable ? Heaven is honourable. Who is wise ? Heaven is wise. And, so, righteousness assuredly comes from Heaven. And the gentlemen of the world who desire to do righteousness therefore must obey the will of Heaven.

What is the will of Heaven that is to be obeyed ? It is to love all the people in the world universally. How do we know it is to love all the people in the world universally ? Because (Heaven) accepts sacrifices from all. How do we know Heaven accepts sacrifices from all ? Because from antiquity to the present day there is no distant or isolated country but what feeds oxen and sheep, dogs and pigs with grass and grains, and prepare clean cakes and wine to worship God, hills and rivers, and the spirits. So we know Heaven accepts sacrifices from all. Accepting sacrifice from all, Heaven must love them all. Take the lords of Ch'u and Yüeh for instance. The lord of Ch'u accepts offering from all within the four borders of Ch'u, therefore he loves the people of Ch'u. And, the lord of Yüeh accepts offering from all within the four borders of Yüeh, therefore he loves the people of Yüeh. Now Heaven accepts offering from all the world and so I know Heaven loves all the people in the world.

That Heaven loves all the people of the world is proved not only by this. In all the countries in the world and among all the people who live on grains, the murder of one innocent individual brings down one calamity. Now who is it that murders the innocent ? It is man. Who is it that sends down the calamity ? It is Heaven. If Heaven really did not love the people, why does Heaven send down calamities for the murder of the innocent ?

Furthermore, Heaven loves the people dearly, Heaven loves the people inclusively. And this can be known. How do we know Heaven loves the people ? Because of the certain reward to the good and punishment to the evil from the virtuous (Heaven). How do we know the virtuous (Heaven) certainly rewards the good and punishes the evil ? I know this from the (examples of) the sage-kings of the Three Dynasties. Anciently, the sage-kings of the Three Dynasties, Yao, Shun, Yü, T'ang, Wen, and Wu, loved the world universally and proceeded to benefit them. They converted the desires of the people and led them to worship God, hills and rivers, and the spirits. Heaven was pleased because they loved what it loved and benefited what it would benefit, and bestowed rewards upon them, placing them on the throne, crowning them emperor, upholding them as the standard, and calling them sage-kings. Here we have the proof of reward of the good.

Anciently, the wicked kings of the Three Dynasties, Chieh, Chow, Yu, and Li, hated all the world and proceeded to oppress them. They converted the desires of the people and led them to blaspheme against God, hills and rivers, and the spirits. Heaven was offended because they hated those whom Heaven loved and oppressed those whom Heaven would benefit, and Heaven decreed punishments upon them, letting fathers and sons be scattered, their empire be put to an end, their state be lost to them, and capital punishment fall upon them. Thereupon, the multitudes in the world condemned them, the condemnation lasting all through the ten thousand generations, the people calling them wicked kings. Here we have the proof of punishment of the evil.

Those gentlemen of the world who desire to do righteousness have only to obey the will of Heaven. To obey the will of Heaven is to be universal and to oppose the will of Heaven is to be partial (in love). According to the doctrine of universality righteousness is the standard; in the doctrine of partiality force is the basis of government. What is it like to have righteousness as the basis of government? The great will not attack the small, the strong will not plunder the weak, the many will not oppress the few, the clever will not deceive the ignorant, the honoured will not disdain the humble, the rich will not mock the poor, and the young will not rob the old. And the states in the empire will not ruin each other with water, fire, poison, and weapons. Such a regime will be beneficial to Heaven above, to the spirits in the middle sphere, to the people below. Being beneficial to these three it is beneficial to all. This is called the virtue of Heaven; whoever practises this is a sage, magnanimous, gracious, and righteous, loyal, affectionate, and filial, and all such good names in the world will be gathered and atrributed to him. Why so? Because such conduct is in accordance with the will of Heaven.

Now, what is it like to have force as the basis of government? The great will attack the small, the strong will plunder the weak, the many will oppress the few, the clever will impose upon the ignorant, the honoured will disdain the humble, the rich will mock the poor, and the young will rob the old. And the states in the empire will ruin each other with water, fire, poison, and weapons. Such a regime will not be helpful to Heaven above, to the spirits in the middle sphere, or to the people below. Not being helpful to these three, it is not helpful to any. This is called the enemy of Heaven. He who practises this is a bad man, not magnanimous, not gracious, and unrighteous, disloyal, unaffectionate, and unfilial, and all such evil names in the world are gathered and attributed to him. Why so? Because such conduct is in opposition to the will of Heaven.

Hence Motse established the will of Heaven as his standard, just as the wheelwright uses his compasses and the carpenter uses his square as their standards. The wheelwright with his compasses and the carpenter with his square can judge the circularity and the squareness of objects. Similarly, with the will of Heaven as the standard, Motse can tell that the gentlemen of the world are far from righteousness.

How do we know the gentlemen of the world are far from righteousness? For, the lords in the large states compete in saying: "Being a big state, if I do not attack the small states, in what way am I big?" Therefore they mustered their warriors and soldiers, and arranged their boat and chariot forces to attack some innocent state. They broke into its borders, cut down its fields, felled its trees, tore down its inner and outer city walls, and filled up its moats and ditches, burned its ancestral temples and seized and killed its sacrificial victims. Of the people the strong were killed, the weak were brought back in chains and ropes. The men were turned into servants and grooms and prisoners. The women were made to be waitresses (to pour wine). Yet, the warring lord did not even know that this is unmagnanimous and unrighteous. He announced to the neighbouring lords: " I have attacked a state, defeated an army, and killed so many generals." And the neighbouring lords did not know that this is unmagnanimous and unrighteous either, but with furs and silk sent envoys to offer congratulations. And the warring lords were even doubly ignorant of its being unmagnanimous and unrighteous. They recorded it on the bamboos and silk and kept them in the archives so that the descendants would imitate their royal ancestors, saying: " Why not let us open up the archives and let us learn of the achievements of our ancestors ? " Then they would surely not learn : " Such and such is the regime of Wu," but would learn : " I have attacked states, reversed armies, and killed so many of their generals." Now that the warring lords do not understand this to be unmagnanimous and unrighteous, and neighbouring lords do not understand this to be unmagnanimous and unrighteous, therefore attacks and assaults go on generation after generation without end.

What do I mean when I say people do not understand things of importance but understand trifles ? Supposing some one entered the orchard and garden of another and took the other's peaches and prunes, melon and ginger, he will be punished by the superior when caught and condemned by the public when heard of. Why ? Because he did not share the toil but takes the fruit and appropriates what is not his. How much more is this true with him who jumps over another's fence and maltreats the children of the other ; of him who digs into another's storehouse and carries away

the other's gold, jade, silk, and cloth ; of him who breaks
into another's fold and steals the other's oxen and horses ;
and of him who kills an innocent person ?   In the government
of the lords of to-day all—from the one who kills an innocent
person to the one who jumps over another's fence and maltreats
the other's children, who digs into another's warehouse
and carries away his gold, jade, silk and cloth, who breaks
into another's fold and steals his oxen and horses, and who
enters another's orchard and garden and takes his peaches
and prunes, melons and ginger—all these are punished quite
the same as they would be even in the government of Yao,
Shun, Yü, T'ang, Wen, and Wu.   Now the lords and chiefs
in the world all attack and absorb others. This is a thousand
and ten thousand times worse than killing one innocent
individual, a thousand and ten thousand times worse than
jumping over another's fence and maltreating his children
or digging into another's storehouse and carrying away
his gold, jade, silk, and cloth, a thousand and ten thousand
times worse than breaking into another's fold and stealing
his oxen and horses, or entering another's orchard and garden
and taking his peaches and prunes, melons and ginger. Yet,
they claim it to be righteous.

Motse said : This is meant to confuse us. And is this
at all different from confusion in the distinctions between
black and white, and sweet and bitter ? Suppose a man
who upon being shown a little blackness says it is black,
but upon being shown much blackness says it is white. He
will have to admit that his sight is confused and that he
cannot tell the difference between black and white. Suppose
a man when served with a little bitter says it is bitter, but

when served with much bitter says it is sweet. Then he
will have to admit that his taste is impaired and that he
cannot tell the difference between sweet and bitter. In the
government of the present lords, the murderer of an individual
is imprisoned by the state. This [1] . . . But the murderer
of many men of the neighbouring states is upheld as righteous.
How is this different from confusing the distinction between
black and white and sweet and bitter ?

Therefore Motse established the will of Heaven to be
the standard. Not only Motse established the will of Heaven
to be the standard, it is also the theme of an ode in the
" Ta Ya " [2] among the books of the ancient kings: " God
said to King Wen, ' I cherish your intelligent virtue. It
was not proclaimed with much noise or gesture. It was not
modified after the possession of the empire. Instinctively
and naturally submissive to the scheme of God.' " [3] This
is to proclaim that King Wen used the will of Heaven as
standard and was submissive to God's scheme. If the gentlemen of the world really desire to practise magnanimity and
righteousness and be superior men, seeking to attain the way
of the sage-kings on the one hand and to procure blessings
to the people on the other, they must not neglect to understand the will of Heaven. The will of Heaven is truly the
standard of righteousness.

[1] The major part of the sentence is lost.

[2] " Ta Ya " is the general title of the collection of the major odes of
the Dynasty of Chou, in *Shih Ching*.

[3] *Supra*, p. 147, note 1.

BOOK VIII

CHAPTER XXXI

On Ghosts (III)

Motse said : With the passing of the sage-kings of the Three Dynasties, the world lost its righteousness and the feudal lords took might as right. The superior and the subordinates are no longer gracious and loyal; father and son, elder and younger brother are no longer affectionate and filial, brotherly and respectful, virtuous and kind. The rulers do not attend diligently to government and the artisans do not attend earnestly to their work. The people practise immorality and wickedness and become rebellious. Thieves and bandits with weapons, poison, water, and fire hold up innocent travellers on the highways and the bypaths, robbing them of their carts and horses, coats and fur coats, to enrich themselves. All these start therewith (with the passing of the sage-kings). And so the world falls into chaos.

Now what is the reason for this confusion ? It is all because of the doubt of the existence of the ghosts and spirits, and the ignorance of their being able to reward virtue and punish vice. If all the people in the world believed that the spirits are able to reward virtue and punish vice, how could the world be in chaos ? Those who deny the existence of spirits proclaim : " Of course there are no spirits." And from morning till evening they teach this doctrine to the people of the empire. They bewilder the people, causing them all to doubt the existence of ghosts and spirits. In this way the empire becomes disorderly. Therefore Motse said : If the rulers and the gentlemen of the world really desire to procure benefits for the empire and remove its calamities they must understand whether ghosts and spirits exist or not.

Since we must understand whether ghosts and spirits exist or not, how can we find out ? Motse said : The way to find out whether anything exists or not is to depend on the testimony of the ears and eyes of the multitude. If some have heard it or some have seen it then we have to say it exists. If no one has heard it and no one has seen it then we have to say it does not exist. So, then, why not go to some village or some district and inquire ? If from antiquity to the present, and since the beginning of man, there are men who have seen the bodies of ghosts and spirits and heard their voice, how can we say that they do not exist ? If none have heard them and none have seen them, then how can we say they do ? But those who deny the existence of the spirits say : " Many in the world have heard and seen something of ghosts and spirits. (Since they vary in their testimony,) who are to be accepted as really having heard and seen them ? " Motse said : As we are to rely on what many have jointly seen and what many have jointly heard, the case of Tu Po is (to be accepted).[1]

King Hsuan of Chou (827–783 B.C.) put his minister Tu Po to death though he was innocent. Tu Po remarked : " The king puts me to death while I am innocent. If man loses his

---

[1] In the following paragraphs Motse cites a number of cases to support the existence of spirits. Most of the persons and occasions mentioned are historical, but the details seem to have come from the fairy tales current at his time.

consciousness after his death, then all is over. If I shall still retain my consciousness after death I shall let the king know of this within three years." In three years, King Hsuan assembled the feudal lords at P'u T'ien. There were several hundred carts. Attendants numbered by the thousand and the multitude covered the fields. At noon Tu Po in red garments and headgear appeared riding in a plain chariot drawn by a white horse, holding a red bow and carrying red arrows. He pursued King Hsuan and shot him on his chariot. The arrow pierced his heart and broke his back. He fell and died prostrate. At the time all the people of Chou who were there saw it and those far away heard of it, and it was recorded in the Spring and Autumn [1] of Chou. Rulers instructed their ministers with it and fathers warned their sons with it, saying : " Be careful, be respectful. All who kill the innocent are speedily and severely visited by misfortune and punished by the ghosts and spirits like this." Judging from what is recorded here, how can we doubt that ghosts and spirits exist ?

Not only does the record in this book prove it to be so. Formerly, Lord Mu of Ch'in [2] (about 640 B.C.) was once in the temple at noon. A spirit entered and alighted. He had the face of a man but the body of a bird. His attire was plain and dark. His appearance was dignified. Seeing him Lord Mu became afraid and was rushing away. The spirit said : " Do not be afraid. God cherishes your intelligent virtue, authorizing me to prolong your age by nineteen years, and ordaining your state to be prosperous and your descendants

---

[1] Spring and Autumn was then not a proper name, title of the annals of Lu written by Confucius, but a common name for any annals.

[2] The text says Lord Mu of Cheng. But the incident historically belongs to Lord Mu of Ch'in.

to be many and not to lose Ch'in." Lord Mu saluted him repeatedly and bowed, saying : " May I ask the name of my god ? " He answered : " I am Kou Mang." If we are to accept what Lord Mu of Ch'in had seen personally as reliable, then how can we doubt that spirits and ghosts exist ?

Not only does the record in this book [1] prove it to be so. Formerly Lord Chien of Yen (about 500 B.C.) put his Minister Chuang Tse Yi to death while he was innocent. Chuang Tse Yi remarked : " The lord puts me to death though I am innocent. If man loses his consciousness after death then all is done. If I shall still retain my consciousness after death, I shall let the Lord know of this within three years." In a year, Yen [2] was going to repair to Tsu. Such ceremonies were the occasions of large assemblages of men and women. At noon Lord Chien was riding on the road to Tsu. Chuang Tse Yi carried a red staff and struck and prostrated him. At the time all the people of Yen who were there saw it and all those who were far away heard of it. And it was recorded in the Spring and Autumn of Yen. The feudal lords circulated the news around, and remarked : " So speedy and severe are the misfortunes and punishment from the spirits and ghosts upon him that kills the innocent." Judging from the record in this book, how can we doubt that spirits and ghosts exist ?

Not only does the record in this book prove it to be so. Anciently, in the reign of Lord Wen of Sung, whose name was Pao (610–589 B.C.), there was a master of ceremonies by the name of Kuan Ku. While he was working in the temple,

---

[1] That is, the historical record of Ch'in.

[2] Yen is the name of the state, but here means the lord of Yen, who is its representative.

a wizard [1] carrying a cane appeared and said to him : " Kuan Ku, why don't the jades and stones measure up to the standard, and why are the cakes and wine unclean, and the victims imperfect and not fat, and the sacrifices not in season? Did you do this or did Pao do this ? " Kuan Ku answered : " Pao is still small and in his swaddle-clothes. What does he have to do with this ? It is all done by the official in charge, Kuan Ku." Thereupon the wizard lifted his cane and struck him, prostrating him on the altar. At the time those people who were present all saw it and those far away heard of it. And it was recorded in the Spring and Autumn of Sung. The feudal lords circulated the news and remarked : " So speedy and severe is the punishment from spirits and ghosts to him who is not reverent in performing sacrifices ! " Judging from the record of this book, how can we doubt that spirits and ghosts exist ?

Not only does the record in this book prove it to be so. Formerly the Lord Chuang of Ch'i (794–731 B.C.) had two ministers, Wang Li Kuo and Chung Li Chiao, who were engaged in a lawsuit. For three years no judgment could be reached. The Lord of Ch'i thought of putting both of them to death, but was afraid to slay the innocent; he thought of acquitting both of them but was afraid to let loose the guilty. So he let them provide a lamb and take oath on the altar of Ch'i. The two men agreed to take the oath of blood. The throat of the lamb was cut and its blood sprinkled on the altar. The case of Wang Li Kuo was read all through. But before half of the case of Chung Li Chiao was read, the lamb arose and butted at him, broke his leg and prostrated him on

---

[1] The wizard 祩 子 is here represented as a medium of the spirits.

the altar. At the time all the people of Ch'i who were present
saw it, and those far away heard of it. It was recorded in the
Spring and Autumn of Ch'i. The feudal lords circulated the
news around and remarked : " So speedy and severe is the
punishment from spirits and ghosts to him that takes an oath
in insincerity ! " Judging from the record in this book, how
can we doubt that spirits and ghosts exist ?

Therefore Motse said : One may not act disrespectfully
even in woods, valleys, or solitary caves where there is no
man. Spirits and ghosts are watching everywhere.

Those who deny the existence of spirits ask : " Are the
senses of hearing and sight of the multitude sufficient to
decide a doubt ? How can people strive to be learned gentlemen while they continue to trust the senses of hearing and
sight of the multitude ? "

Motse said : If the senses of hearing and sight of the
multitude are thought to be not trustworthy, we may ask
if such men like the sage-kings of the Three Dynasties, Yao,
Shun, Yü, T'ang, Wen, and Wu, are trustworthy ? Of course,
about this all people above the mediocre will say such men
like the ancient sage-kings of the Three Dynasties, Yao, Shun,
Yü, T'ang, Wen, and Wu, are trustworthy. If the ancient
sage-kings of the Three Dynasties are trustworthy, we may
review some of their deeds.

In ancient times, having captured Yin and punished Chow,
King Wu let the feudal lords share in the worship (of the
ancestors of Yin). Those more closely related were to partake
in the temple sacrifices and those less closely related in the
outdoor sacrifices. So then King Wu must have believed
there were spirits and ghosts, therefore after capturing Yin

and punishing Chow he let the feudal lords share in the worship. If there were no spirits and ghosts why did King Wu assign the duties of worship ?

Not only does the deed of King Wu prove it to be so. When the ancient sage-kings distributed rewards it must be before their ancestors. When they meted out punishments it must be before the altar. Why are the rewards distributed before the ancestors ? To submit their fairness. Why are punishments meted out before the altar ? To submit their justice.

Not only does the record in that book prove it to be so. On the day when the ancient sage-kings of the Three Dynasties of Yü, Hsia, Shang, and Chou[1] first established their empire and built their capitals, they invariably chose the central altar on which to build the ancestral temple. They would pick out the luxuriant and elegant among the trees to plant in the temple of agriculture. They would select the affectionate and filial, virtuous and kind among the elders of the country to be masters of ceremonies. They would pick out the victims among the six animals by their fatness, perfection, and the colour of their wool. The jades and stones were to be appropriate in material and satisfactory in measurement. And the cakes and wine were to be prepared with the most fragrant and yellow grain, and so the quality of cakes and wine would vary with the abundance of the year. This is to say, in the government of the ancient sage-kings, spirits and ghosts had priority over the people. Before the offices and courts were completely established, the sacrificial vessels and sacrificial robes must have been

[1] The " Three Dynasties " denotes only the last three.

all stored in the storehouse, the masters and attendants of ceremonies must have all been installed in court, and the victims must be kept apart from the original flock. Since the government of the ancient sage-kings was like this, the ancient sage-kings must have believed in the existence of spirits and ghosts.

Deep was their own interest in the welfare of ghosts and spirits. Yet they were afraid their descendants might not understand it. Thus they recorded it on bamboos and silk to bequeath to them. Fearing that these might rot and disappear so that the descendants might not learn it, they engraved it on plates and cups and cut it in metals and stones. They feared also that the descendants might not be reverent and obtain blessing, and so among the books of the ancient kings and the records of sages testimonies to the existence of ghosts and spirits occur time and again even on a single foot of silk or a single sheet in the books. Why was this ? Because the sage-kings were interested in it. Those who deny the existence of spirits are opposing the interest of the sage-kings, and such is not the way of the superior man.

Those who deny the existence of spirits might say : "Among the books of the ancient kings not a foot of silk or a sheet is found which testifies to the existence of ghosts and spirits once and again. Then where are these testimonies ? "

Motse replied : They are found (for instance) in the "Ta Ya" of the books of Chou. "Ta Ya" tells : "The rule of King Wen over the people pleased Heaven. Although Chou is an old country, it is newly commissioned by Heaven. Chou does not appear showy. The commission from God does not appear to be seasonable. King Wen reached high and low, he was on the left and the right of God. How active was King Wen! He dispensed his intelligent virtue without ceasing." [1] If ghosts and spirits do not exist, then how could King Wen be "on the left and right of God" since he wàs already dead? Here we have a testimony of ghosts in the book of Chou.

If there are testimonies only in the books of Chou and none in those of Shang still it could not be reliable. But we find among the books of Shang the following: "Oh! Anciently, before Hsia was visited by misfortune, of the various animals and insects and even birds none deviated from their proper course. As to those who have faces of men, who dare be divergent in heart? Even the hills and rivers ghosts and spirits dared not be insurgent." [2] If one is respectful and sincere one could maintain harmony in the world and stability to the lower earth. Now it was to assist Yü that hills and rivers ghosts and spirits dared not be insurgent. Here we have a testimony of ghosts in the book of Shang.

If there are testimonies of ghosts only in the books of Shang and none in those of Hsia it is still not reliable. But we have "Speech at Kan" [3] among the books of Hsia running thus: "In the midst of the war at Kan the Emperor called

---

[1] This quotation is from the ode "Wen Wang" in the collection "Ta Ya" in *Shih Ching*. It is a eulogy of the career of King Wen. Legge's rendition is found in vol. iv, pp. 427–8.

[2] The quotation is from the "Instructions of E" in *Shu Ching*. But the two texts differ widely in wording. For comparison, see Legge, vol. iii, pp. 193–4.

[3] The text says "Speech of Yü". Some ancient writers seem to use both titles for the same work. In the present text of *Shu Ching* the essay is called "Speech at Kan".

the six associates to receive instructions in the headquarters.
He said : ' The Prince of Hu violated the five elements and
disused the three calendars.   Heaven decreed to exterminate
his life ! '   And he continued : ' At noon I shall grapple
with the Prince of Hu for the fate of the day.   But (mind
you), you ministers and people, it is not because I covet
their land and treasures.   I am only carrying out the punishment in obedience to Heaven.   If you on the left do not
do your part on the left you will be disobeying my orders ;
if you on the right do not do your part on the right you will
be disobeying my orders ; if you charioteers do not manage
your horses according to orders you will be disobeying
my orders.   And rewards will be distributed before my
ancestors and punishments will be meted out before the
altar.' " [1]   Why   were   rewards   distributed   before   the
ancestors ?   To submit their fairness.   Why were punishments meted out before the altar ?   To submit their justice.
Because the ancient sage-kings must reward virtue and punish
vice with ghosts and spirits, they distributed rewards before
the ancestors and meted out punishments before the altar.
And here we have a testimony of ghosts in the books of Hsia.

Now, first in the books of Hsia and next in the books of
Shang and Chou, testimonies to the existence of ghosts and
spirits occur again and again.   What is the reason for this ?
Because the sage-kings were interested in it.   Judging
from the records of these books, how can we doubt that there
are ghosts and spirits ?

[1] This is almost the whole of the " Speech at Kan ". But in many places
the texts differ greatly.   For the text in *Shu Ching*, see Legge, vol. iii,
pp. 152-5.

Anciently, on the propitious day of ting mao,[1] Chou offered thanksgiving to Earth and the Four Quarters, and their ancestors. They did this to prolong their age. If there were no ghosts and spirits, how could their age be prolonged ?

Motse said : As to the fact that ghosts and spirits can reward virtue as well as punish vice, if it could be proclaimed to the whole country and to all the people it would really be a source of orderliness in the country and blessing to the people. The corruption of the officials in their public charges and the immorality among men and women will all be seen by ghosts and spirits. The vice of those who, with weapons, poisons, and water and fire, waylay innocent travellers and rob them of their carts and horses, coats and fur coats to enrich themselves will be seen by ghosts and spirits. Thereupon the officials will not dare be corrupt in office, withholding reward when they find the virtuous or withholding punishment when they find the wicked. And those among the people who commit vice and cruelties and with weapons, poisons, and water and fire waylay the innocent travellers, robbing them of their carts and horses, coats and fur coats to enrich themselves—all these will be no more. And the world will have order. Really the intelligence of the ghosts and spirits cannot be combated. Even in solitary caves, big ponds, woods and valleys, the ghosts and spirits are watching. And the punishments from ghosts and spirits cannot be evaded. Even wealth and great numbers, daring and strength, strong armour and

---

[1] Ting Mao 丁 卯 is the name of the day according to the Chinese calendar then in use. For a discussion of the Chinese Sexagenary Cycle, see p. 229, note 1.

sharp weapons, the punishment of ghosts and spirits will frustrate.

If this is doubted, look at the story of the ancient King Chieh of Hsia. He was an emperor in honour and possessed the whole empire in wealth. He cursed Heaven and blasphemed against the spirits above and destroyed the multitudes below.[1] Thereupon Heaven commissioned T'ang to carry out the judicious punishment. With nine chariots [2] T'ang arranged the Bird Formation and the Wild Goose March. He climbed the Ta Tsan [3] and scattered the forces of Hsia and entered its land. And he captured T'uei Yi Ta Hsi. Now, King Chieh of Hsia was an emperor in honour and possessed the whole empire in wealth. In his service was the man of great daring and strength, T'uei Yi Ta Hsi, who had torn apart a buffalo alive. He could kill a man at the move of a finger, and the number of those killed amounted to a million, and they were thrown into lakes and mountains. Yet, for all this, Chieh could not evade the punishment from ghosts and spirits. This is why I say even wealth and numbers, daring and strength, strong armour and sharp weapons cannot combat the punishment from ghosts and spirits.

Not only is this so. Anciently, King Chow of Yin was also an emperor in honour and possessed the whole empire in wealth. He cursed Heaven and blasphemed against the

---

[1] There is a sentence in the text following this which does not seem to make any sense as it stands, and is therefore not translatable. In Chinese it is 祥 上 帝 伐 元 山 帝 行.

[2] Each chariot unit consists of twenty-five men. It seems it should be " ninety " chariots instead of "nine".

[3] Ta Tsan is most likely the name of a pass.

spirits above and destroyed the multitudes below. He exposed the aged and murdered the children, tortured the innocent, and opened a pregnant woman. The common people and the widows and the widowers cried aloud, but were not heard. Thereupon Heaven commissioned King Wu to carry out the judicious punishment. With a hundred selected chariots and four hundred warriors King Wu appointed his officials and reviewed his forces. He battled the armies of Yin in the Wilderness of Mu. He captured Fei Chung and E Lai, and the multitude deserted and ran away. King Wu rushed into the palace.[1] He executed Chow and hung him on a red ring with his crimes published on a white flag, to punish him for the feudal lords in the empire. Now King Chow of Yin was an emperor in honour and possessed the whole empire in wealth. He had men of such daring and strength as Fei Chung,[2] E Lai,[2] and Duke Hu of Ch'ung,[2] who could kill a man at the move of a finger ; and the number of those killed amounted to a million, and they were thrown into the lakes and mountains. Yet with all these Chow could not evade the punishment from the ghosts and spirits. This is why I say even wealth and numbers, daring and strength, strong armour and sharp weapons cannot frustrate the punishment from ghosts and spirits.

Moreover, Ch'in Ai has said : " No virtue is too small ; no extermination of a lineage is too big." This is to say, in distribution of rewards by ghosts and spirits no man is too insignificant to be rewarded for his virtue. And in the

---

[1] The four words following this do not seem to have anything to do with this narration. In Chinese they are 萬 年 梓 株.

[2] All these men are the vicious associates of Chow.

meting out of punishments by ghosts and spirits no man is too great to be punished.

Those who deny the existence of spirits say, "If one does not work for the blessing of one's parents but work for their destruction, would one still be a filial son ? "

Motse explained : The ghosts and spirits of all times may be divided into spirits of Heaven, spirits of hills and rivers, and ghosts of men after their death. It is true that there are sons who die before their fathers, and younger brothers before their elder brothers. But, as the saying in the world goes : " He who is born first dies first." So then those who die first would be the mother if not the father, and the elder sister if not the elder brother.

At any rate, we should prepare clean cakes and wine reverently to do sacrifice. If ghosts and spirits do exist, then it is to serve father and mother, elder sisters and elder brothers with food and drink. Is not this a great blessing ? If ghosts and spirits did not exist it would seem to be a waste of the material for the cakes and wine. But such use is not just to throw it into the ditch or gully. For the relatives from the clan and friends from the village and district can yet eat and drink them. So, even if there were really no ghosts and spirits, a sacrifice will yet gather together a party and the participants can enjoy themselves and befriend the neighbours. Those who hold there are no ghosts say : " Of course there are no ghosts and spirits and therefore I should not expend my wealth on the cakes and wine and victims. This is not because I am miserly about my wealth on the cakes and wine and victims. But (because I do not see) what I can accomplish with it." This is opposed to the records of the sage-kings above and opposed to the practice among the filial sons among the people. Yet they claim to be superior men in the empire. This is no way to be superior men. But Motse said : For me to offer sacrifice is not to throw it into the ditch or the gully. It is to bless the ghosts above and gather a party and enjoy ourselves and befriend the neighbours below. And if spirits exist, I would be serving my father and mother and brother with food. Is this not a great blessing in the world ?

Therefore Motse said : If the rulers and the gentlemen of the world really desire to procure benefits for the world and eliminate its calamities they must believe in and teach the existence of ghosts and spirits. This is the way of the sage-kings.

CHAPTER XXXII

Condemnation of Music (I)

Motse said : The policy of the magnanimous will pursue what procures benefits of the world and destroy its calamities. If anything, when established as a law, is beneficial to the people it will be done ; if not, it will not be done. Moreover, the magnanimous in their care for the world do not think of doing those things which delight the eyes, please the ears, gratify the taste, and ease the body. When these deprive the people of their means of clothing and food, the magnanimous would not undertake them. So the reason why Motse condemns music is not because that the sounds of the big bell, the sounding drum, the ch'in [1] and the she [1] and the yü [2] and the sheng [2] are not pleasant, that the carvings and ornaments are not delightful, that the fried and the broiled meats of the grass-fed and the grain-fed animals are not gratifying, or that the high towers, grand arbours, and quiet villas are not comfortable. Although the body knows they are comfortable, the mouth knows they are gratifying, the eyes know they are delightful, and the ears know they are pleasing, yet they are found not to be in accordance with the deeds of the sage-kings of antiquity and not to contribute to the benefits of the people at present. And, so, Motse proclaims : To have music is wrong.

[1] Ch'in 琴 is a Chinese horizontal psaltery of five, six, or seven strings, according to the fashion of the dynasty. She 瑟 is a psaltery of twenty-five strings.

[2] Yü 竽 is a hand organ of thirty-six reed pipes. Sheng 笙 is one of seventeen bamboo pipes.

Now the rulers construct musical instruments as an under-taking of the state. They cannot be produced as easily as by evaporating water or digging into the earth. Inevitably heavy taxes have to be collected from the people to obtain sounds of the big bell, the sounding drum, the ch'in and the she, and the yü and the sheng. The ancient sage-kings had, indeed, collected heavy taxes from the people to build boats and vehicles. But when they were completed, and when the people asked : " What use have we for these ? " the answer was : " The boats are to be employed on water and the vehicles on land, so that the gentlemen can rest their feet and the labourers can rest their shoulders and backs." Thus the people contributed their money and dared not grumble about it. This was because the boats and vehicles contributed to the benefit of the people. If the musical instruments also contribute to the benefit of the people, even I shall not dare condemn them. Thus if the musical instruments are as useful as the boats and carts with the sage-kings, even I shall not dare condemn them.

There are three things that the people worry about, namely, that the hungry cannot be fed, that the cold cannot be clothed, and that the tired cannot get rest. These three are the great worries of the people. Now suppose we strike the big bell, beat the sounding drum, play the ch'in and the she, and blow the yü and the sheng, can the material for food and clothing then be procured for the people ? Even I do not think this is possible. Again, every large state now attacks small states and every large house molests small houses. The strong plunder the weak, the many oppress the few, the clever deceive the stupid and the honoured disdain the humble.

And bandits and thieves rise all together and cannot be suppressed. But can the chaos in the world be put in order by striking the big bell, beating the sounding drum, playing the ch'in and the she, and blowing the yü and the sheng? Even I do not think it is possible. Therefore Motse said: The levy of heavy taxes on the people to construct the big bell, the sounding drum, the ch'in and the she, and the yü and the sheng, is not at all helpful in the endeavour to procure the benefits of the world and destroy its calamities. Therefore Motse said: To have music is wrong.

As the rulers look down from a high tower or in a grand arbour, a bell is just like an inverted ting.[1] If it is not struck wherefrom would come the pleasure? Therefore it must be struck. To strike it of course the aged and the young would not be employed. For their eyes and ears are not keen, their arms are not strong, and they cannot produce an harmonious tone with varied expression. So, those in the prime of life must be employed because their eyes and ears are keen, their limbs strong, their voices harmonious and varied in expression. If men are employed it interferes with their ploughing and planting. If women are employed it interferes with their weaving and spinning. Now, the rulers take to music and deprive the people of their means of clothing and food to such an extent! Therefore Motse said: To have music is wrong.

Now when the big bell, the sounding drum, the ch'in and the she, and the yü and the sheng are provided it is yet no pleasure for the lords alone to listen to the playing. Therefore they must enjoy it with either the common people or

---

[1] Ting 鼎 is a tripod-shaped sacrificial vessel.

the gentlemen. If with the gentlemen, it will interfere with their attending to government. If with the common people it will interfere with their work. Now the rulers take to music and deprive the people of so many of their opportunities to produce food and clothing ! Therefore Motse said : It is wrong to have music.

Formerly, Lord K'ang of Ch'i (404–379 B.C.) loved music and dancing. The dancers were not to wear garments of coarse cloth or to eat husks and bran. For if food and drink are not dainty the appearance and complexion will not be enjoyable. And if clothing is not elegant the body and the movement will not be delightful. Therefore their food must consist of grain and meat and their clothing must be made of silk and embroidery. They did not produce material of clothing and food at all, but lived on others all the time. Hence Motse said : Now the lords take to music and deprive the people of so many of their opportunities to produce food and clothing ! Therefore Motse proclaimed : To have music is wrong.

Also, man is different from birds and beasts and insects. The birds, beasts, and insects have their feathers and furs for coats and fur coats, have their hoofs and claws for sandals and shoes, and have water and grass for drink and food. Therefore the male do not sow seeds or plant trees, neither do the female weave or spin, yet food and clothing are provided. Now, man is different from these. Those who exert themselves will live. Those who do not exert themselves cannot live. When the gentlemen do not attend to government diligently, the jurisdiction will be in chaos. When the common men do not attend to work, supply will not be sufficient.

If the gentlemen of the world should doubt my word, let us enumerate the several duties in the world and see the harm music does (to them) : For the rulers to go to court early and retire late to listen to lawsuits and attend to government is their duty. For the gentlemen to exhaust the energy of their limbs and employ fully the wisdom of their minds to attend to the court within and to collect taxes without from passes, markets, and products from mountains, woods, and water and fields in order to fill up the granaries and the treasury is their duty. For the farmers to set out early and come back late, to sow seeds and plant trees in order to produce a large quantity of soy beans and millet[1] is their duty. For the women to rise up at dawn and retire in the night to weave and spin in order to produce much silk, flax linen, and cloth is their duty. Now if the rulers should love music and listen to it, they would not be able to go to court early and retire late to listen to lawsuits and attend to government. Then the country would be in chaos and the state would be in danger. If the gentlemen should love music and listen to it, they would not be able to exhaust the energy in their limbs and employ fully the wisdom in the mind to attend to court within and collect taxes without from passes and markets and products from mountains, woods, water, and fields to fill up the granaries and the treasury. Then the granaries and the treasury would not be filled. If the farmers should love music and listen to it, they would not be able to set out early and come back late to sow seeds and plant trees and produce a large quantity of soy beans and millet. Then the soy beans and millet would

---

[1] Soy beans and millet are used to represent grains in general.

not be sufficient.   If the women should love music and listen
to it, they would not be able to rise up at dawn and retire
in the night to weave and spin and produce much silk, flax
linen, and cloth.   Then cloth and linen will not be sufficient.
If it is asked what is it that interfered with the rulers'
attending to government and the common man's attending
to work ? it must be answered, music.   Therefore Motse said :
To have music is wrong.

How do we know it is so ?   It is found in the " Code of
Punishment of T'ang " among the books of the ancient kings.
This proclaims : " To have constant dancing in the palace
is called the witch's pleasure." [1]   As to its punishment, a
gentleman will be fined six hundred and forty [2] pieces of silk,
a common man will be let go free.   Again, " Ah ! How much
is the dancing.   His word is all known.   God does not bless
him, therefore the nine districts [3] are lost to him.   God
does not favour him, therefore He visited him with various
curses.   His family must be destroyed too." [4]   Now the
reason that the nine districts are lost to him (Chieh of Hsia)
lies in his attention to embellish music.

---

[1] There is not such a book as the " Code of Punishment of T'ang " in *Shu
Ching*.   A passage resembling this quotation is found in the " Instructions of E ".   According to Legge, vol. iii, p. 196, it runs thus : " He laid
down the punishments for officers and warned them who were in authority,
saying : ' If you dare to have constant dancing in your palaces, and drunken
singing in your chambers—that is called sorcerers' fashion.' "

[2] The correctness of this number is doubtful.

[3] The Empire at the time consisted of nine districts.

[4] Cf. Legge, vol. iii, p. 198, "Instructions of E " in *Shu Ching*.   The two
texts differ widely both in wording and even in meaning.   Competent
critics agree in thinking the text in *Motse* is more likely the original *Shu
Ching* text.

Quoting *Wu Kuan*[1]: " Ch'i [2] thereupon abandoned himself to lust and music. He drank and ate in improper places. Ding ding, dong dong went the wood winds and percussion instruments in harmony. He indulged in drinking and ate in improper places. Brilliantly went on the dancing. It reached the hearing of Heaven, and Heaven was not pleased." So, it was not pleasing to Heaven above and not beneficial to the people below.

Therefore Motse said : If the gentlemen really desire to procure benefits for the world and destroy its calamities they cannot but prohibit such a thing as music.

[1] *Wu Kuan* is a book that is no more existent.
[2] Ch'i is the son of Yü and second Emperor of Hsia Dynasty.

BOOK IX

CHAPTER XXXV

ANTI-FATALISM (I)

Motse said : At present, in governing the states the rulers all desire to have their countries wealthy, their population large, and their administration orderly. But instead of wealth they obtain poverty, instead of an increase they obtain a decrease in population, instead of order they obtain chaos ; i.e. they lose what they like but obtain what they dislike. What is the reason for this ? Motse said : It is due to the large number of fatalists among the people.

The fatalists say : "When fate decrees that a man shall be wealthy he will be wealthy ; when it decrees poverty, he will be poor ; when it decrees a large population, this will be large ; and when it decrees a small population this will be small ; if order is decreed, there will be order ; if chaos, there will be chaos. If fate decrees old age, there will be old age ; if untimely death, there will be untimely death. Even if a man sets himself against his fate, what is the use ? " With this doctrine the rulers are urged above and the people are kept away from their work below. Hence the fatalists are unmagnanimous. And their doctrines must be clearly examined.

Now, how is this doctrine to be examined ? Motse said : Some standard of judgment must be established. To expound a doctrine without regard to the standard is similar to determining the directions of sunrise and sunset on a revolving

potter's wheel. By this means the distinction of right
and wrong, benefit and harm, cannot be known. Therefore
there must be three tests. What are the three tests ? Motse
said : Its basis, its verifiability, and its applicability. How
is it to be based ? It should be based on the deeds of the
ancient sage-kings. How is it to be verified ? It is to be
verified by the senses of hearing and sight of the common
people. How is it to be applied ? It is to be applied by
adopting it in government and observing its benefits to the
country and the people. This is what is meant by the three
tests of every doctrine.

Some of the gentlemen of the world assume there to be
fate. Now let us examine the deeds of the sage-kings. In
ancient times, the confusion produced by Chieh was replaced
by an orderly government by T'ang, the chaos of Chow was
turned into order by King Wu. The times did not alter and
the people did not change, yet under Chieh and Chow the
world was chaotic and under T'ang and Wu it was orderly.
Can it be said that there is fate ?

But the gentlemen of the world still assume that there
is fate. Now let us look at some of the writings of the early
kings. The writings of the early kings that were issued to
the whole country and distributed among the people were
the laws 憲. Did any of the laws of the early kings ever
say : " Blessing cannot be invoked and disaster cannot be
avoided ; reverence will not do any good and cruelty will
not do any harm " ? The standards according to which
lawsuits were tried and punishments were meted out
were the codes of punishment 刑. Did any of the codes of
punishment of the early kings say : " Blessing cannot be

invoked and disaster cannot be avoided ; reverence will not do any good and cruelty will not do any harm " ? The inspiration by which the armies were organized and the soldiers were commanded to advance or to retreat came from the declarations 誓. Did any of the declarations of the early kings say : " Blessing cannot be invoked and disaster cannot be avoided ; reverence will do no good and cruelty will do no harm " ? Motse said : I have not enumerated the good books of the empire completely. As they cannot be exhaustively enumerated, I limit myself to the most prominent ones, namely, the three [1] above mentioned. And try as we may, we cannot find any belief in the doctrine of fatalism. Should it not then be abandoned ?

To adopt the fatalists' doctrine is to overthrow righteousness in the world. To overthrow righteousness in the world will establish fate, which is a temptation to the people. And to offer people temptation is to destroy the people. Now, why is it that we desire righteousness to be with the superiors ? Because when the righteous are in authority, the world will have order, God, hills and rivers, and the spirits will have their chief sacrificer, and the people will be visited by the great blessings therefrom. How do we know ? Motse said : In ancient times, T'ang was given a fief at Po. Making allowance for the irregular boundary lines, his land amounted to about a hundred li square. He worked with the people for mutual love and reciprocal benefit, and shared with them what was in abundance. And he led his people to

---

[1] The text has " five " which should be " three " as in the translation. The three refer to the laws, the codes of punishment, and the declarations. The error might be due to copying 五, five, for 三, three, by some copyist.

reverence Heaven and worship the spirits. Thereupon, Heaven and the spirits enriched him, the feudal lords befriended him, the people loved him, and the virtuous came to him. Within a single generation he ruled over the empire and headed the feudal lords.

Again in ancient times, King Wen was assigned to the state of Ch'i Chou. Making allowance for the irregular boundary lines, his land amounted to about a hundred li square. He worked with his people for mutual love and reciprocal benefit. So those near him enjoyed his government and those distant submitted themselves to his virtues. All who heard of King Wen rose up and rushed over to him. The stupid and insolent and those weak in limbs remained where they were and complained : " Why not let the land of King Wen extend to this place. Wouldn't I then also be a subject of King Wen ? " Thereupon Heaven and the spirits enriched him, the feudal lords befriended him, the people loved him and the virtuous came to him. Within a single generation he ruled over the whole empire and headed the feudal lords. As we have said : When the righteous are in authority the world will have order, God, hills and rivers, and the spirits will have their chief sacrificer, and the people will be visited by the great benefits therefrom. And this is how we know it to be so.

The ancient sage-kings published laws and issued orders to be standards of reward and punishment, and to encourage the virtuous and to obstruct the evil. And so the people were filial to their parents at home and respectful to the elders in the village or the district. They observed propriety in conduct, moderation in going out and coming in, and decency between men and women. And when they were made to look after the court they would not steal, when they were made to defend a city they would not raise an insurrection. When the lord met with death they would commit suicide, and when the lord was banished they would follow him. This is what the superior will reward and what the people will applaud. Now, the fatalists say : " Whoever is rewarded by the superior is destined to be rewarded. It is not because of his virtue that he is rewarded." Under these conditions the people would not be filial to their parents at home, and respectful to the elders in the village or the district. They would not observe propriety in conduct, moderation in going out and coming in, or decency between men and women. And, if they were made to look after the court they would steal, if they were made to defend a city they would raise an insurrection. If the lord met with death they would not commit suicide, and if the lord were banished they would not accompany him. This is what the superior will punish, and what the people will condemn. The fatalists say : " Whoever is punished by the superior is destined to be punished. It is not because of his vice that he is punished." Believing in this, the ruler would not be righteous, the minister would not be loyal, the father would not be affectionate, the son would not be filial, the elder brother would not be brotherly, and the younger brother would not be respectful. The unnatural adherence to this doctrine is responsible for pernicious ideas and is the way of the wicked.

Now how do we know fatalism is the way of the wicked ? In ancient times, the miserable people indulged in drinking and eating and were lazy in their work. Thereupon their food and clothing became insufficient, and the danger of hunger and cold was approaching. They did not acknowledge: " I was stupid and insolent and was not diligent at work." But they would say : " It is but my lot to be poor." The ancient wicked kings did not control the sensuality of their ears and eyes and the passions of their mind. They did not follow their ancestors and so they lost their country and ruined their state. They did not know that they should confess : " I am stupid and insolent and was not diligent in attending to government." But they would say : " It is but my fate to lose it." The " Announcement of Chung Hui " says: " I have heard that the man of Hsia issued orders, pretending them to be fate of Heaven. God was displeased and destroyed his forces." [1] This tells how T'ang showed Chieh's belief in fate to be wrong. " The Great Declaration " says : " Chow became insolent and would not worship God and pushed away the ancestors and spirits without offering them sacrifices. And he said : ' Fortune is with my people,' and neglected and betrayed his duty. Heaven thereupon deserted him and withdrew its protection." [2] This tells how King Wu showed Chow's belief in fate to be wrong.

If the doctrine of the fatalist were put to practice, the superiors would not attend to government and the subordinates would not attend to work. If the superior does not attend to government, jurisdiction and administration will be in chaos. If the subordinates do not attend to work, wealth will not be sufficient. Then, there will not be wherewith

---

[1] Chung Hui is a minister of T'ang. The text in *Shu Ching* is somewhat different. Cf. Legge, vol. iii, p. 179.

[2] *Supra*, p. 149, and note 1 same page.

to provide for the cakes and wine to worship and do sacrifice to God, ghosts and spirits above, and there will not be wherewith to tranquillize the virtuous of the world below; there will not be wherewith to entertain the noble guests from without, and there will not be wherewith to feed the hungry, clothe the cold, and care for the aged and weak within. Therefore fatalism is not helpful to Heaven above, nor to the spirits in the middle sphere, nor to man below. The eccentric belief in this doctrine is responsible for pernicious ideas and is the way of the wicked.

Therefore Motse said : If the gentlemen in the world really desire to have the world rich and do not want to have it poor, desire to have it orderly and dislike to have it in confusion, the doctrine of fatalism must be rejected. It is a great calamity to the world.

CHAPTER XXXVI

ANTI-FATALISM (II)

Motse said : To make any statement or to publish any doctrine, there must first be established some standard of judgment. To discuss without a standard is like determining the directions of sunrise and sunset on a revolving potter's wheel. Even skilful artisans could not get accurate results in that way. Now that the truth and error (of a doctrine) in the world is hard to tell, there must be three tests. What are the three tests ? They are the test of its basis, the test of its verifiability, and the test of its applicability. To test the basis of a doctrine we shall examine the will of Heaven and spirits and the deeds of the sage-kings. To test its verifiability we shall go to the books of the early kings. As to its applicability it is to be tested by its use in the administration of justice and government. These then are the three tests of a doctrine.

Among the gentlemen of to-day some think there is fate, some think there is no fate. That I am able to judge whether there is fate or not is by the sense testimony of the multitude. If some have heard it and some have seen it I shall say there is fate. If none has heard it, if none has seen it, I shall say there is no fate. Why not then let us inquire into the sense testimony of the people ? From antiquity to the present, since the beginning of man, has any seen such a thing as fate, or has heard the sound of fate ? Of course, there is none. If the common people are considered stupid and their senses of hearing and sight unreliable, then why not inquire into the recorded statements of the feudal lords ? But from antiquity to the present, since the beginning of man, has any of them heard the sound of fate or seen such a thing as fate ? Of course, none of them has. Again, why not let us inquire into the deeds of the sage-kings ? The ancient kings promoted the filial sons and encouraged them to continue to serve their parents, and respected the virtuous and gentle and encouraged them to continue to do good. They published their orders to instruct (the people), and made reward and punishment fair to encourage (the good) and obstruct (the evil). In this way confusion could be reduced to order and danger could be converted to peace. If anyone doubts this, let us recall : In ancient times the confusion of Chieh was reduced to order by T'ang, and that of Chow by King Wu. Now, the times did not change and the people did not alter. Yet when the superior changed a regime the subordinates modified their conduct. Under T'ang and Wu it was orderly, but under Chieh and Chow it was disorderly. Hence peace and danger, order and disorder, all depend on the government of the superior. How can it be said everything is according to fate ? So, assertions about there being fate are quite false.

The fatalists tell us : " This doctrine has not been invented by us in a late generation. Such a doctrine has appeared and been handed down since the Three Dynasties. Why do you, sir, now oppose it ? " (In answer,) Motse asked : Was it from the sages and good men of the Three Dynasties or from the wicked and the vicious of the Three Dynasties that the fatalistic doctrine came ? How can we find this out ? In the beginning secretaries and ministers were careful in speech and intelligent in conduct.   They could persuade their ruler above and instruct the people below.   Thus they obtained reward from their ruler and applause from the people.   And the fame of those secretaries and ministers has come down to the present day.   The whole world remarks : "This is the result of endeavour."   And it will never say : [1] "I see fate there."

On the other hand, the wicked kings of the Three Dynasties did not control the lust of their ears and eyes and did not restrain the passions of their heart.   When they went out they indulged in racing, hunting, and trapping.   When they stayed indoors they revelled in wine and music.   They did not attend to the government of the country and of the people, but they did much that was of no use.   They oppressed the people, causing the subordinates not to love their superior.   Hence the country became empty and without any future, and they themselves were in punishment and disaster.   But they would not confess and say :   "I am stupid and insolent and poor in administering the government."   But they would say :   "It is but my fate to perish."   Even the miserable people of the Three Dynasties were like this.   Within they could not well serve their parents, without they could not well serve their ruler.   They disliked politeness and frugality but liked licence and ease. They indulged in drinking and eating and were lazy.   The means of food and clothing became insufficient and they placed themselves in danger of hunger and cold.   They would not confess :   "I am stupid and insolent and was not diligent

---

[1] The first part of the following sentence seems to be missing.

at work." But they would say : " It is but my fate to be poor." Such, then, also were the miserable people of the Three Dynasties.

Fatalism has been glossed over and taught the stupid people. This was of great concern to the sage-kings, and they put it down on the bamboos and silk and cut it in metals and stone. Among the books of the early kings, " The Announcement of Chung Hui " says : " I have heard the man of Hsia issue orders, pretending them to be fate of Heaven. God was displeased and destroyed his forces." [1] This shows how King Chieh of Hsia believed in fate and how both T'ang and Chung Hui thought it to be wrong. Among the books of early kings " The Great Declaration " says : " Chow became insolent and would not worship God, and pushed away the ancestors and spirits without offering them sacrifices. And he said : ' Fortune is with my people,' and neglected and betrayed his duty. Heaven thereupon deserted him and withdrew its protection." [2] This shows how Chow believed in fate and how King Wu proclaimed it to be wrong with " The Great Declaration ". Again, " The Three Dynasties and Hundred States " [3] says : " Do not place too much faith in the fate in Heaven." So " The Three Dynasties and Hundred States " also says there is no fate. Also " Shao Kung " [3] in the same way discredits the belief in fate. It says : " Assuredly there is no fate in Heaven. Let us two not teach false doctrines. (One's destiny) does

---

[1] *Supra*, p. 187, and note 1 same page.

[2] *Supra*, p. 149, and note 1 same page, and p. 187, note 2.

[3] Both " The Three Dynasties and Hundred States " and " Shao Kung " seem to be essays in *Shu Ching* that are now lost.

not come from Heaven, but is shaped by one's self." And
it is said in the odes and books of Shang and Hsia : " Fate
is born of the wicked kings."

So, then, if the gentlemen of the world desire to distinguish
right and wrong, benefit and harm, fate of Heaven must be
strenuously discredited.   To hold there is fate is the great
disaster of the world.   And therefore Motse refuted it.

CHAPTER XXXVII

ANTI-FATALISM (III)

Motse said : In order to expound a doctrine there must be established some standard of judgment. To expound without a standard is similar to determining the directions of sunrise and sunset on a potter's wheel that is turning. I should think even such obvious distinctions as that between the directions of sunrise and sunset cannot be thus determined. Therefore every doctrine must stand three tests. What are the three tests ? They are the test of its basis, the test of its verifiability, and the test of its applicability. How is it to be based ? It is to be based on the deeds of the early sage-kings. How is it to be verified ? It is to be verified by the testimony of the ears and eyes of the multitude. How is it to be applied ? It is to be applied by being adopted in government and its effects on the people being shown. These are called the three tests.

When the ancient sage-kings of the Three Dynasties, Yü, T'ang, Wen, and Wu, ruled, they said : " We must promote the filial sons and encourage them in serving their parents, and we must honour the virtuous and good men and instruct them in doing good." In this way they administered the government and published instructions, rewarded the good and punished the evil. It seems, in this way the confusion in the world could be reduced to order, and the danger of the state could be transformed into safety. If this is doubted, (let us recall) : In ancient times, the disorder of Chieh was reduced to order by T'ang, that of Chow was reduced to order by King Wu. Then the times did not change nor did the people alter. Yet when the superior changed regime the subordinates modified their conduct. With Chieh and Chow the world was chaotic, under T'ang and Wu it became orderly. That the world became orderly was due to the endeavour of T'ang and Wu. That the world was chaotic was due to the sin of Chieh and Chow. Judging from this, safety and danger, order and chaos all depend on the way the superior conducts the government. How can it be said, there is fate ? In ancient times when Yü, T'ang, Wen, and Wu ruled the empire, they said : " We must feed the hungry, clothe the cold, give the weary rest, and the disturbed peace." Thus their good name was heard all over the world. Can this be ascribed to fate ? It is really due to endeavour. The virtuous and gentle of to-day respect virtue and pursue the ways and means (to benefit the world). Hence they are rewarded by the rulers above and praised by the people below. And their good name is heard all over the world. Can this be ascribed to fate ? This is also due to their endeavour.

Now, were those who believed in fate the sages of the Three Dynasties or the wicked of the Three Dynasties ? Judging from the nature of this doctrine, it could not be the sages of the Three Dynasties, but must be the wicked that believed in fate. The ancient wicked kings of the Three Dynasties, Chieh, Chow, Yu, and Li, were honoured as emperors and possessed the whole world in wealth. Yet they could not control the sensuality of their ears and eyes, but gave rein to their passions. Going out they would race, hunt, and trap. Staying indoors they revelled in wine and music. They did not attend to the government of the country and the people, but did much that was of no use. And they oppressed and violated the people. Thus they lost their ancestral temple.[1] They would not confess: "I am insolent and stupid. I did not attend to government diligently." But they would say: "It is but my fate that I lose it." Even the insolent people of the Three Dynasties were like this. They could not well serve their parents and their lord. They greatly hated politeness and frugality but liked licence and ease. They indulged in eating and drinking and were lazy at work. Their means of clothing and food became insufficient, and they incurred the danger of hunger and cold. They would not confess: "I am stupid and insolent. I am not diligent in my work." But they also said: "It is but my fate that I am poor." Thus the insolent people of the Three Dynasties also believed in fate.

The ancient wicked kings originated it and the miserable people practised it. It was shaking the convictions of the multitudes and converting the stupid. And this was already of great concern to the ancient sage-kings. They put it down on the bamboos and silk and cut it in metal and stone and engraved it on dishes and cups to be handed down to their descendants. In what books are they embodied? "Tsung Teh"[2] of Yü says: "When promises are not fulfilled even a subject of Heaven will not be protected. When one has touched the evil star, Heaven will visit him with its curse. When one is not careful about one's conduct, how can fate

---

[1] The loss of the ancestral temple is a figure for the loss of the empire, for it is the last thing that one can afford to be captured by the enemy.

[2] "Tsung Teh" seems to be a lost essay in *Shu Ching*.

of Heaven protect him ? " " The Announcement of Chung
Hui " says : " I have heard that the man of Hsia issued
orders, pretending them to be fate of Heaven. God was
displeased and destroyed his armies." [1] He made use of
what did not exist as if it had existed, and therefore it was
called pretension. If he declared to be existent what really
existed, how would this be pretension ? In ancient times,
Chieh believed in fate and acted accordingly. T'ang here
showed it to be wrong through " The Announcement of
Chung Hui ". " The Great Declaration " says : " Therefore the Prince Regent Fa [2] said : ' Ah, my lords, Heaven
blesses the virtuous. Its way is clear. Example need not
be sought far. It is in the King of Yin. He claimed each
man had his own fate, worship should not be practised,
sacrifices were of no avail, and wickedness could do no harm.
God withdrew his blessing and the nine districts are lost to
him. God is not pleased and is visiting him with ruin.
Hence it is that our Chou (the dynasty, the empire) is given
by the Great God.' " [3] That is, Chow believed in fate and
acted accordingly. King Wu refuted him in " The Great
Declaration ". So, why not examine the records of Yü,
Hsia, Shang, and Chou, and see that all of them held there
is no fate ? How would you account for this ?

And Motse said : In expounding a doctrine or elaborating
a system the gentlemen of the world should not do it just to
exercise their voice and tongue and practise their lips. It

---

[1] *Supra*, p. 187, and note 1 same page; p. 192, and note 1 same page.

[2] Fa is the personal name of King Wu.

[3] According to the present text of *Shu Ching*, this quotation is a collection
of sentences scattered all through the two parts of "The Great Declaration ". For reference, see Legge, vol. iii, pp. 291, 294, 295–6, 297.

must aim at being applied in the government of the country, the district, and the people. Now the rulers go to court early and retire late, hearing lawsuits and attending to government and meting out justice for the whole day, and dare not be negligent. Why do they do this? They think diligence will bring about order, and negligence chaos; diligence will produce safety, and negligence danger. Therefore they dare not be negligent. The ministers and secretaries exhaust the energy in their limbs and stretch the wisdom of their minds within to look after the court and without to collect taxes from passes, markets, and products from mountains, woods, ponds, and fields to fill the treasury, and dare not be negligent. Why do they do this? They think diligence will procure honour and negligence dishonour; diligence will procure glory and negligence disgrace. Therefore they dare not be negligent. The farmers set out at daybreak and come back at dusk, diligently sowing seeds and planting trees to produce much soy beans and millet, and dare not be negligent. Why do they do this? They think diligence will result in wealth, and negligence in poverty; diligence will produce plenty, and negligence famine. Therefore they dare not be negligent. The women get up at dawn and retire in the night, diligently weaving and spinning to produce much silk, flax linen, and cloth, and dare not be negligent. Why do they do this? They think diligence will produce wealth and negligence poverty; diligence will produce warmth and negligence cold. Therefore they dare not be negligent.

Now, if they should believe in fate and behave accordingly, the rulers would be negligent in hearing lawsuits and attending to government; the ministers and secretaries would be negligent in attending to court; the farmers would be negligent in sowing seeds and planting trees; the women would be negligent in weaving and spinning. When the rulers are negligent in hearing lawsuits and attending to government and the ministers and secretaries in attending to court, then I should think the world would be in chaos. When the farmers are negligent in sowing seeds and planting trees and the women in weaving and spinning, then according to my opinion clothing and food for the world will be insufficient. As to the result of the application of the doctrine of fatalism to the government of the empire, to worship Heaven and the spirits above with it Heaven and the spirits will not be pleased, and to nurture the people below with it they will not be benefited but will be demoralized and cannot be employed. And, within, defence will not be strong, and, without, attack will not be victorious. And that for which the wicked kings of the Three Dynasties, Chieh, Chow, Yu, and Li, lost their country and ruined their state was just this (doctrine).

Therefore Motse said: If the gentlemen of the world really desire to procure benefits for the world and destroy its calamities they cannot but vigorously refute the doctrine of fatalism. For, fatalism was an invention of the wicked kings and the practice of miserable men. It was not a doctrine of the magnanimous. Therefore those who practise magnanimity and righteousness must examine it and vigorously refute it.

CHAPTER XXXIX

ANTI-CONFUCIANISM (II) [1]

The Confucianist says: Love among relations should depend upon the degree of relationship, and honour to the virtuous should be graded.[2] This is to advocate a discrimination among the near and the distant relations and among the respectable and the humble. But, according to his code of propriety: Mourning for the death of the parent should be three years; for the wife or the eldest son three years; for an uncle, a brother, or one of the other sons, a year; and for a near relative, five months. If the periods are based on the degree of relationship, evidently mourning for the closer relative should be longer and for the more distant shorter. Thus the wife and the eldest son are the same as the parents (in nearness). If the periods are based on degrees of respect which are severally due then it means that the wife and the eldest son are respected as much as the parents, and the uncles and brothers are placed on the same level with the other sons. What perversity can be greater than this!

When his parent dies he first lets him lie there without

---

[1] There are just two records of this discourse. Record (I) is lost. The statements in the present record are not introduced with " Motse said ", and the composition and style show remarkable variation from the other books. And the confused dates and facts of the historical allusions show this chapter to be written at a much later date. It evidently is not the recorded words of Motse. The master might have had the main ideas, but they were certainly put into the present exaggerated form by someone else.

[2] This Confucian tenet is found in *The Doctrine of the Mean* 中庸, Legge, vol. i, p. 270 : " The decreasing measures of the love due to relatives, and the steps in the honour due to the worthy, are produced by the principle of propriety."

dressing him for burial. He climbs on the roof, looks into
the well, reaches into the rat holes, and searches in the
washing basins to look for the dead man.[1] Assuming that the
man still exists this procedure is certainly stupid. If he does
not exist this insistent search is the height of hypocrisy.

When a Confucianist takes a wife,[2] he has to escort her
in person, dressed in ceremonial garments as a servant.
He drives the cart himself, as if waiting on a revered parent.
The dignity and solemnity of the marriage ceremony compare
with that of sacrifice and worship. High and low are turned
upside down. Father and mother are disobeyed. Parents
are brought down to the level of the wife and the wife is exalted
to interfere with service to parents. Can such conduct be
called filial ? The Confucianist tells us : " A wife is taken
to share in continuing the worship and sacrifice (to ancestors)
and the son will attend to the ancestral temple, therefore
they are highly regarded." We answer him : This is all false
representation. For, his brothers attend to the ancestral
temple for tens of years. Yet when they die he will mourn
for them only one year. The brothers' wives continue the
worship and sacrifice of his ancestors. Yet, there is no
mourning (upon their death) whatsoever. Then the three
years' mourning for the death of his wife and eldest son is
evidently not for the reason of their attending to the ancestral
temple and continuing the worship and sacrifice. Now,
to be partial to one's wife and son is already quite wayward.
Yet the Confucianist pretends it to be for the sake of the

---

[1] These ceremonies are not found in *Li Chi*.

[2] This description is based on the " Ceremony of the Scholar's Wedding ",
in *Yi Li*.

parents. This is partiality to the most favourite but neglect
of the most important. Isn't this great perversity ?

Further, he holds tenaciously to the dogma of fate and
argues : " Old age or early death, poverty or wealth, safety
or danger, order or chaos are destined by the fate of Heaven
and cannot be modified. Failure or success, reward or
punishment, luck or adversity, are all settled ; the wisdom
and power of man can do nothing." When the different
officers believe this they will neglect their several duties.
When the common people believe this they will neglect
their work. Lax government will lead to disorder ; inefficient
agriculture will lead to poverty. And poverty is the root
of disorder and insurrections. Yet the Confucianists
take this teaching about fate to be the Tao and
the principle of life. This is to destroy the people of the
empire.

Moreover, the Confucianist glosses over the elaborate
ceremonials and music to make man extravagant ; he extends
mourning and pretends grief to cheat his parents. He
introduces fate and causes poverty, and lives in idleness.
He overthrows the fundamentals and avoids work, and is
indolent and proud. Self-indulgent in drinking and eating
and too lazy to work, he often suffers from hunger and cold
and is in danger of freezing and starvation, without ability
to avert them. He behaves like a beggar ; grasps food like
a hamster, gazes at things like a he-goat, and rises up like
a wild boar. The gentlemen all laugh at him. He becomes
angry and exclaims : " What does the undisciplined man
know about the good Confucianist ? " In spring and summer
he begs for grains. When the five grains are all gathered in

he resorts to the funerals.[1] All the sons and grandsons are taken along and are filled with drink and food. It is sufficient for him to manage but a few funerals. He depends on others' houses for his wealth and uses others' fields to uphold his dignity. When a death takes place in a rich family he will rejoice greatly, for it is his opportunity for clothing and food.

The Confucianist says : " The superior man must be ancient in mode of speech and in dress before he can be magnanimous." We answer him : The so-called ancient speech and dress were all modern once. When the ancients first used that speech and wore that dress they would not be superior men (according to the Confucianists' criteria). Do you therefore mean to say that one has to wear the dress of the non-superior man and speak the speech of the non-superior man before he can be magnanimous ?

Again, the Confucianist says : " The superior man conforms to the old but does not make innovations." [2] We answer him : In antiquity Yi invented the bow, Yü invented armour, Hsi Chung invented vehicles, and Ch'iao Ch'ui invented boats. Would he say, the tanners, armourers, and carpenters of to-day are all superior men, whereas Yi,

---

[1] In the Chinese socio-cosmic religion there is no priesthood. The whole nation was represented by the Emperor at the periodical sacrifices to Heaven, Earth, and the other gods and spirits. Marriage and funeral ceremonies, however, are not without religious sanctity and significance, and these occasions are usually dignified by the presence of some official or scholar. The charge here made against the Confucianist seems to be a caricature of this practice.

[2] Cf. Confucian *Analects,* Book VII, Legge, vol. i, p. 59, " The master said : ' A transmitter and not a maker, believing in and loving the ancients, I venture to compare myself with our old Pang.' "

Yü, Hsi Chung, and Ch'iao Ts'ui were all ordinary men ? Moreover, some of those whom he follows must have been inventors. Then his instructions are after all the ways of the ordinary men.

Again he says: "When the superior man is victorious he does not pursue the fleeing enemy. When the enemy is kept at bay he does not shoot. When the enemy retreat he will help them pushing their carts." We answer him : If the magnanimous are here referred to, they have no occasion for strife. The magnanimous remind each other of the principle of right and wrong and of what is to be accepted and what is to be rejected. He who has no cause follows him who has it. He who has no knowledge follows him who has knowledge. Running short of argument he would acknowledge defeat, seeing good he would be converted. How can there be any strife ? If the contestants are both wicked, though the victor does not pursue the fleeing enemy, though he does not shoot the enemy at bay, though he helps pushing the enemy's carts in retreat—though he does all these, still he cannot be a superior man. On the other hand, suppose a sage starts out to destroy a curse on behalf of the empire. He raises an army to punish the wicked and cruel state. When he is victorious, let us suppose him to follow the Confucian way and command his army : " Don't pursue the fleeing enemy. Don't shoot when the enemy is at bay. Help them pushing the carts when they retreat." The wicked men will thus be set free and the curse of the world will not yet be removed. This is to harm the parents of the multitudes and greatly to ruin the world. Nothing can be more unrighteous !

Again the Confucianist says : " The superior man is like a bell. It will sound when it is struck. It will remain silent when it is not struck." We answer him : The magnanimous, in serving his superior, should be loyal, and in serving his parents, should be filial. When there is excellence (in the superior) he should adore, when there is fault he should give counsel. This is the way of a minister. Now, if one sounds only when struck, and remains silent when not struck, then he will hide his knowledge and spare his efforts, waiting to be questioned before he answers. Even if there is some great advantage at stake to the lord or parents, he will not speak up without being asked. And, if a great invasion or insurrection is approaching or a conspiracy is afoot, and none know it but he ; yet even in the presence of his lord and parents he will not speak up without being questioned. What a criminal, producing confusion ! Such a man will not be loyal as a minister, filial as a son, respectful in serving an elder brother or gentle in treating the people.

When benefit is in sight, the only fear should be that counsel may be late. When the ruler starts something not beneficial, one should fold his hands high on the breast and look down and utter with difficulty : " This I have not learned." Upon emergency one should withdraw and set out on a long journey.[1] For, every principle, doctrine, and standard of magnanimity and righteousness are to be used on the large scale to rule men and on the small scale to hold office ; widely, to exercise a universal influence and, narrowly, to cultivate one's person. What is not righteous should

[1] The text of the last two sentences is very faulty. This interpretation is correct in principle.

not be tolerated ; what is not according to principle should
not be practised: One should endeavour to procure benefits
for the empire directly and indirectly, avoiding that which
brings no profit : such is the way of the superior man. But
what we hear of the conduct of K'ung Mo [1] is diametrically
opposed to this.

Lord Ching of Ch'i asked Yentse : " What kind of a man
is Confucius ? " Yentse answered not. The Lord reiterated
the question and there was still no answer. Lord Ching
said : " Many have told me about K'ung Mo and all said he
was a virtuous man. Now that I am asking you about him, why
should you not answer ? " Yentse replied : " Ying [2] is not wise
and cannot know virtuous men. Yet Ying has heard that a
virtuous man must be one who, upon entering a state, will
endeavour to bring about friendly relations between the
ruler and the ministers and dissolve the grudges between
superior and subordinates. This man Confucius once visited
the state of Ching. He heard of the plans of Duke Po and
told them to Shih Ch'i. As a result, the lord almost perished
and Duke Po was executed.[3] Ying has also heard that the
virtuous man does not obtain confidence of the superior by
flattery or that of the subordinates by threat. If his counsels
are listened to by the lord they will benefit the people, if his
instructions are followed by the subordinates they will

[1] The family name of Confucius is K'ung, and his own name is Ch'iu.
But the sage has become too great to be called by name, and so his own name
was changed to Mo, meaning " somebody ". Confucius is a Latinized
transliteration of K'ung Fu Tse, meaning K'ung the revered teacher.

[2] Ying is the " first name " of Yentse. Yen is his " last name ".

[3] This historical incident happened long after Yen Ying's time. It must
have been wrongly put into his mouth by the author. The account is very
much distorted at the expense of Confucius, too.

benefit the superior. His speech is plain and easy to understand and his conduct is plain and easy to follow. His righteous conduct enlightens the people and his thoughtful counsel convinces the lord and his ministers. Now, this man Confucius with elaborate plans conspired with the rebels and with devious plots committed depravity. To persuade the subordinates to plot against their superior and tell the ministers to assassinate their lord is not the conduct of a virtuous man. To enter a country and join with its traitors is not akin to the righteous. To urge those who are known to be disloyal to revolt does not fit the way of the magnanimous. Plotting against one at a distance and condemning one behind his back, his conduct enlightening not the people and his counsel convincing not the lord—how Confucius is different from Duke Po, your servant Ying does not see. This is why I did not answer you." Lord Ching said : " Oh ! I have been benefited. If it were not for you, I would never in my life understand K'ung Mo to be of the same kind as Duke Po."

K'ung Mo visited the state of Ch'i and saw Lord Ching. Lord Ching was pleased and was going to assign Ni Hsi [1] to him. He told Yentse about it. Yentse said : " Please do not. A scholar of his school would sit crouching and take things easy, therefore he cannot be made to teach the subordinates. He likes music and will corrupt the people, and therefore cannot be trusted to govern. He believes in fate and will neglect his duty, therefore he cannot be given an office. He lays emphasis on mourning and makes much of grief, therefore he cannot be made to take care of

---

[1] Ni Hsi is the name of a place, probably a district.

the people. He will be formal in dress and affected in manners, therefore he cannot lead the multitudes. K'ung Mo dresses elaborately and puts on adornments to mislead the people, promotes music and dancing to attract the multitudes, performs elaborate ceremonies of going up and coming down the steps, and practises the etiquette of rushing and soaring [1] to dazzle the multitudes. With all his extensive learning he cannot plan for the world ; with all his laborious thought he cannot help the people. A whole lifetime cannot exhaust his learning ; the grown man cannot observe his ceremonies ; and even the wealthy cannot enjoy his music. He elaborates and adorns his improper ways to keep the lords busy ; he profusely furnishes sounds and music to corrupt the people. His principles cannot instruct the world ; his learning cannot lead the multitudes. Now you, my lord, commission him to change the customs of Ch'i. It really is not the way to lead a country and bring forward the multitudes." The Lord said : " This is well."

Thereupon the Lord gave him valuable gifts but retained the commission, received him with respect but did not inquire into his teaching. K'ung Mo became angry, angry with Lord Ching and Yentse. So, he placed Ch'ih Yi Tse P'i in the following of T'ien Ch'ang,[2] and communicated his plans to Huitse [3] of the South City. Then he returned to Lu. Before long, Ch'i desired to attack Lu. He remarked to

---

[1] A ceremonious movement of the body during which the arms are so placed as to imitate the wings of a bird.

[2] T'ien Ch'ang is a general of Ch'i.

[3] Huitse is a follower of T'ien Ch'ang.

Tse Kung[1]: "Oh, Ts'e[1]! now is the time to do the great deed." Thereupon he sent Tse Kung to Ch'i and, through the introduction of Huitse of the South City, saw T'ien Ch'ang. Tse Kung persuaded him to attack Wu (instead of Lu). He also told Kao Kuo Pao Yen[2] not to interfere with T'ien Ch'ang's insurrection. Then he went on and persuaded Yüeh to attack Wu. For three years, both Ch'i and Wu were threatened with ruin. The bodies of those killed amounted to hundreds of thousands. And this was the revenge of K'ung Mo.[3]

K'ung Mo was once the Chief Justice of Lu. But he abandoned the cause of the lord and entered the service of Chi Sun.[4] Chi Sun was the Chancellor of Lu but deserted his trust and ran away.[5] As he was trying to force the gate against the guards, K'ung Mo lifted the beam (for him).

Once, K'ung Mo was in straits between Ts'ai and Ch'en[6] having only vegetable soup without even rice to eat. After ten days of this, Tse Lu[7] cooked a pig for him. K'ung Mo did not inquire whence the meat came, and ate. Tse Lu

---

[1] Tse Kung is one of the seventy-two best disciples of Confucius, and is one of the best known to the later generations. Ts'e is the personal name of Tse Kung, just as Ying is that of Yentse.

[2] Kao Kuo Pao Yen is another general of Ch'i.

[3] According to any historical record this charge is quite false.

[4] Chi Sun is the head of a powerful family in the state of Lu.

[5] This charge is again unfounded.

[6] Mention of this incident in Confucius' life is made in the *Analects*, Book XV, Legge, vol. i, p. 158: "When he was in Chen their provisions were exhausted, and his followers became so ill that they were unable to rise."

[7] Tse Lu is another of the seventy-two best disciples of Confucius. He, like Peter in the Christian Apostolic circle, is noted for courage and straightforwardness.

robbed some one of his garment and exchanged it for wine. K'ung Mo did not inquire whence the wine came, and drank. But when Lord Ai received Confucius, Confucius would not sit on a mat that was not placed straight and would not eat meat that was not cut properly.[1] Tse Lu went to him and asked : " Why the reverse to what you did on the borders of Ch'en and Ts'ai ? " K'ung Mo answered : " Come, let me tell you. Then, our goal was to keep alive. Now our goal is to behave righteously." Now when hunger-stricken he was not scrupulous about the means of keeping alive, and when satiated he acted hypocritically to appear refined. What foolery, perversion, villainy, and pretension can be greater than this !

K'ung Mo was lounging with his disciples. He remarked : " When Shun saw Ku Sou [2] he felt uneasy. The empire at the time must be in danger. Was not Tan, the Duke of Chou, unmagnanimous ? Why did he resign from his public office and retire to his private home ? " [3] This shows K'ung Mo's conduct and the attitude of his mind.

His followers and disciples all imitated him : Tse Kung and Chi Lu [4] assisted K'ung Li [5] and committed high treason against the state of Wei. Yang Huo rebelled against Ch'i.

---

[1] These details occur also in the *Analects*, Book X, in the form of Confucian precepts. Cf. Legge, vol. i, pp. 96, 97.

[2] Ku Sou is the name of Shun's blind father.

[3] These two slighting remarks directed against Shun and Duke Chou would, indeed, constitute an indefensible charge against their author. But that Confucius has made them is most improbable.

[4] Chi Lu is the name of Tse Lu just as Mo Ti is the name of Motse.

[5] K'ung Li is a rebel of the state of Wei. All the other personal names occurring in this paragraph are names of men of the Confucian school.

Fei Kan was entrusted with Chung Mou and became independent.   Ch'i Tiao had a ferocious appearance.   Nothing can be more [1] . . . than this !   Of course the disciples and pupils, following a teacher, will advocate his doctrines and imitate his conduct.   Only, they are not as powerful and not as clever.   Now, since such was the conduct of K'ung Mo, the Confucian scholars are naturally to be objects of suspicion.

[1] A word or a phrase deprecatory in nature following this seems to have been lost.

BOOK XI
CHAPTER XLVI
Keng Chu [1]

Motse was angry with Keng Chutse. Keng Chutse said: "Am I not at all better than others?" Motse said: Suppose I am starting out for T'ai Hang.[2] And a horse and an ox are to pull my cart. Which of them would you urge? Keng Chutse said: "I would urge the horse." Motse asked: Why urge the horse? Keng Chutse said: "Because the horse is capable (of better speed)." Motse said: I also think you are capable (of better things).

Wu Matse [3] questioned Motse: "Which are wiser, the ghosts and spirits or the sages?" Motse said: The ghosts and spirits are wiser than the sages by as much as the sharp-eared and keen-sighted surpass the deaf and blind. In ancient times, Emperor Ch'i [4] of Hsia commissioned Fei Lien to dig minerals in mountains and rivers and cast tings [5] at K'un Wu. He ordered Yi to kill the pheasant to invoke the tortoise of Po Jo,[6] saying: "Let the tings, when completed, be four-legged. Let them be able to cook automatically, without fire, to hide themselves without being

---

[1] Keng Chu or Keng Chutse is the name of a disciple of Motse.

[2] T'ai Hang is a mountain in what is now Honan Province.

[3] Wu Matse might be Wu Ma Ch'i, who was a disciple of Confucius. But it is more likely that this is his son.

[4] Ch'i is the second Emperor of the Dynasty of Hsia, son of Yü. But the story about the nine tings is generally attributed to Yü and not to Ch'i.

[5] Tings 鼎 are tripod-like sacrificial vessels.

[6] Po Jo seems here to be a proper name, name of a place. But commentators differ on this point. Cf. Forke, *Mê Ti*, p. 537.

lifted, and to move themselves without being carried. So that they may be used for the sacrifice at K'un Wu. May our offering be accepted!" Then the oracle was interpreted as saying: "I have accepted the offering. Profuse are the white clouds: one to the south, one to the north, one to the west, one to the east. When the nine tings have been completed, they shall be given over to three empires. When the emperor of Hsia loses them the man of Yin will possess them; when the man of Yin loses them the man of Chou will possess them." Now the transfer from the emperor of Hsia to Yin and Chou took many centuries. Even if the sage planned in counsel with his excellent ministers and superior assistants, could he foresee what would happen after many centuries? Yet the ghosts and spirits can. Therefore we say, the ghosts and spirits are wiser than the sages by as much as the sharp-eared and keen-sighted are than the deaf and blind.

Chih T'u Yü and Hsien Tse Shih [1] asked Motse: "What is the greatest righteousness in conduct?" Motse said: It is like the building of a wall. Let those who can lay the bricks lay the bricks, let those who can fill in the mortar fill in the mortar, and let those who can carry up the material carry up the material. Then the wall can be completed. To do righteousness is just like this. Let those who can argue argue, let those who can expound the doctrines expound the doctrines, and let those who can administer, administer. Then righteousness is achieved.

Wu Matse said to Motse: "Though you love universally the world cannot be said to be benefited; though I do not

[1] Chih T'u Yü and Hsien Tse Shih are two of Motse's disciples.

love (universally) the world cannot be said to be injured. Since neither of us has accomplished anything, what makes you then praise yourself and blame me ? " Motse answered : Suppose a conflagration is on. One person is fetching water to extinguish it, and another is holding some fuel to reinforce it. Neither of them has yet accomplished anything, but which one do you value ? Wu Matse answered that he approved of the intention of the person who fetches water and disapproved of the intention of the person who holds fuel. Motse said : (In the same manner,) do I approve of my intention and disapprove of yours.

Motse had recommended Keng Chutse to Ch'u. Some (other) pupils visited him. They were given only three sheng [1] (of grain) each meal and were not generously entertained. The pupils returned and reported to Motse, saying : " Keng Chutse is not profited by serving Ch'u. When we visited him, we were given only three sheng each meal and were not generously entertained." Motse said : You cannot tell. Shortly after, (Keng Chutse) sent Motse ten chin [2] of silver, saying : " Your junior disciple who dare not die [3] sends herewith ten chin, which I hope you will use." Motse said : So, indeed, we cannot tell.

Wu Matse said to Motse : " For all the righteousness that you do, men do not help you and ghosts do not bless you. Yet you keep on doing it. You must be demented." Motse

---

[1] A sheng 升 now is about a pint. But it was smaller then, perhaps only $\frac{1}{5}$ or $\frac{1}{10}$ as large.

[2] 1 chin 金 = 20 taels, about 27 oz.

[3] The gist of the meaning of this peculiar salutation is that he feels he has been unfilial enough to deserve death.

said : Suppose you have here two employees. One of them works when he sees you but will not work when he does not see you. The other one works whether he sees you or not. Which of the two would you value ? Wu Matse said that he would value him that worked whether he saw him or not. Motse then said : Then you are valuing him who is demented.

A pupil of Tse Hsia [1] asked Motse whether there could be any struggle among the superior men. Motse said : The superior men do not struggle. The pupil of Tse Hsia said : " There is struggle even among the dogs and hogs, how can there be no struggle among men ? " Motse said : What a shame ! T'ang and Wu are praised with words ; but dogs and hogs are brought into comparison in conduct. What a shame !

Wu Matse criticized Motse, saying : " To leave contemporaries alone and to praise the early kings is to praise rotten bones. It is like the carpenter who knows only the decaying lumber but not the living tree." Motse said : Now the world lives because of the instructions of the early kings. And to praise the early kings is to praise the source of life to the world. Not to praise what should be praised is not magnanimous.

Motse said : The jade of Ho, the pearl of Duke Sui, and the nine tings—these are what the feudal lords value as excellent treasures. Can they enrich the country, multiply the people, put the government in order, and place the state in safety ? Of course they cannot. Excellent treasures are to be valued for their efficacy. Now since the jade of Ho, the pearl of Duke Sui, and the nine tings cannot benefit men, then they

---

[1] Tse Hsia is a Confucian disciple.

are not the excellent treasures in the world. On the other hand, if righteousness is employed in the government of the state the population will be increased, the government will be in order, and the state will be secure. The excellent :treasures are to be valued for their efficacy. Now righteousness can benefit men. So then righteousness is the excellent treasure of the world.

Lord Tse Kao of Sheh asked Chung Ni [1] about government, saying : " What is a good governor like ? " Chung Ni answered him that the good governor will attract those who are distant and renew old friendships.[2] Motse heard of it and commented : Lord Tse Kao of Sheh did not put the question right, neither did Chung Ni give the right answer. For, did not Lord Tse Kao of Sheh understand, to be a good governor is to attract the distant and to renew the old friendships ? The question was really how to do this. The answer told only what the inquirer understands but did not tell what he does not understand. Therefore (I say), Lord Tse Kao of Sheh did not put the question right, neither did Chung Ni give the right answer.

Motse said to Prince Wen of Lu Yang [3] : The large states attacking the small states is like the boys playing horse. When the boys play horse, they merely tire out their own

[1] Chung Ni is the tse 字 or second name of Confucius by which he was known to his friends. *Supra*, p. 206, note 1.

[2] This event is also, though somewhat differently, recorded in the *Analects*, Legge, vol. i, p. 269 : " The Duke of Sheh asked about government. The Master said : ' Good government obtains when those who are near are made happy, and those who are far off are attracted.' "

[3] Prince Wen is a Prince of the State of Ch'u, Lu Yang is the Principality assigned to him.

feet. Now, when a large state attacks a small state the farmers of the attacked states cannot cultivate the fields and the women cannot weave. They have to go to the defence. And the farmers of the invading states cannot cultivate the fields and the women cannot weave either. They have to take part in the attack. Therefore (I say) the large states attacking the small states is like the boys playing horse.

Motse said : Doctrines that can be translated into conduct may be taught frequently. Doctrines that cannot be translated into conduct may not be taught frequently. To talk frequently about what cannot be carried out is merely to wear out one's mouth.

Motse sent Kuan Ch'in Ao to recommend Kao Shihtse to Wei. The lord of Wei gave him heavy emoluments and ranked him among the ministers. Kao Shihtse came to court three times and gave all his counsels. But none of them was carried out. So he left for Ch'i where he saw Motse and said : " On your account the lord of Wei gave me heavy emoluments and ranked me among the ministers. I went to court three times and gave all my counsels. But none of them was carried out. So I left. Wouldn't the lord of Wei think I was demented ? " Motse said : If you left because it is in accordance with the Tao,[1] what does it matter even if suspected of being demented ? Anciently, Duke Chou was displeased with Uncle Kuan [2] and resigned from

---

[1] The pregnant word " Tao " 道 is here best understood perhaps as the right way.

[2] Kuan is uncle of the reigning Emperor Ch'eng and brother of Duke Chou.

the Duke's duties and went east to Shang Yen to live. Everybody then said he was demented. But posterity praised his virtue and exalted his name unto this day. Moreover, I have heard, to practise righteousness is not to avoid blame and seek praise. If the resignation is in accordance with the Tao, what does it matter if one is suspected of being demented ? Kao Shihtse said : " How dare Shih leave if it were not in accordance with the Tao ? Formerly, Master, you have said : When there is no Tao in the world, the superior men will not stay in positions of plenty. Now the lord of Wei does not observe the Tao. If I should covet his emoluments and position then I would be living on others as a parasite." Motse was pleased and summoned Ch'intse,[1] telling him : Now, listen, cases of disregard of righteousness for emoluments I have heard of. But disregard of emoluments for righteousness I have seen (only) in Kao Shihtse.

Motse said : When a man calls a gentleman of the present rich while he is poor he becomes angry. Yet, when the man calls him just he will be pleased even though he is unjust. Isn't this perverse !

Kung Mengtse [2] said : " The ancient people had their rules, and they were but three in number." Motse interrupted him, saying : Which ancient people are you talking about that you say have three rules ? You don't understand that people first had [3] . . . .

Some pupils deserted Motse and then returned. (They said :) " How are we to blame ? We deserted late." Motse said :

---

[1] Ch'intse or Ch'in Hua Li is the leading disciple of Motse.

[2] Kung Meng is a Confucianist, probably a pupil of Tsengtse.

[3] The text here is incomplete. It is hard to construe the meaning of the remaining portion.

This is like asking for reward for late desertion in a defeated army.

Kung Mengtse said : " The superior man does not create but transmits." [1] Motse said : Not at all. The most unsuperior men do not transmit the good of old and do not create any good for the present. The less unsuperior men do not transmit the good of old, but will bring out the good which he possesses for the sake of praise. Now to transmit but not to create is not different from creating without transmitting. It seems to me what good there is of old one should transmit it ; what good there is to be for the present, one should institute it, so that the good may increase all the more.

Wu Matse told Motse : " I differ from you. I cannot love universally—I love the people of Tsou better than the people of Ch'u, the people of Lu better than the people of Tsou, the people of my district better than the people of Lu, the members of my family better than the people of my district, my parents better than the other members of my family, and myself better than my parents. This, because of their nearness to me. When I am beaten I feel pain. When they are beaten the pain does not extend to me. Why should I resist what does not give me pain but not resist what gives me pain ? Therefore I would rather have them killed to benefit me than to have me killed to benefit them." Motse said : Is this view of yours to be kept secret or to be told to others ? Wu Matse replied : " Why should I keep my opinion to myself ? Of course I shall tell it to others." Motse said : Then if one person is pleased

[1] *Supra*, p. 203 and note 2 same page.

with you,[1] there will be one person who will desire to kill
you in order to benefit himself.   If ten persons are pleased
with you, there will be ten persons who will desire to kill
you to benefit themselves.   If (the people of) the whole world
are pleased with you, the whole world will desire to kill you to
benefit themselves.   (On the other hand), if one person is not
pleased with you there will be one person who will desire
to kill you as the propagator of a wicked doctrine.   If ten
persons are not pleased with you there will be ten persons
who will desire to kill you as the propagator of an evil doctrine.
If (the people of) the whole world are not pleased with you
the whole world will desire to kill you as the propagator
of an evil doctrine.   (So, then) those who are pleased with
you desire to kill you and those who are not pleased with
you also desire to kill you.   This is to say, what passes out
from your mouth is what kills your body.   Motse continued :
Then, where, after all, does the benefit of your doctrine lie ?
To teach what is not profitable is merely to wear out one's
mouth.

Motse said to Prince Wen of Lu Yang : Here is a man
who has such an abundance of sheep, oxen, and (other)
grass-fed and grain-fed animals that he cannot eat all that
the cooks prepare for him.   (Yet,) when he sees a man baking
cakes, he looks surprised and steals them, saying : " Let
me eat them."   Now, is this due to an unsatisfied appetite
or is he affected with kleptomania ?   Prince Wen of Lu Yang.
replied that he must be suffering from kleptomania.   Motse
said : The fields of Ch'u all lie in waste and cannot be
exhaustively   cultivated.   The   unoccupied   land   amounts

----

[1] You, meaning your doctrine.

to thousands (of mu) and is more than sufficient for cultivation. Yet when it saw the towns of Sung and Cheng, it looked surprised and stole them. Is there any difference between this and the other (case) ? Prince Wen of Lu Yang replied : " This is the same as that. It must be suffering from kleptomania (too)."

Motse said : When Chi Sun Shao and Meng Po Ch'ang were in authority in Lu they could not trust each other. So they took oath at the altar, saying : " May we be harmonious ! " This is like closing one's eyes and praying at the altar : " May I be able to see everything ! " Isn't this unreason ?

Motse said to Lo Hua Li : I have heard you are brave. Lo Hua Li replied : " Yes. When I hear there is a brave man somewhere I always go and kill him." Motse said : The whole world promotes that which it likes and destroys that which it hates. But when you hear of a brave man somewhere you must go and kill him. This is not admiration [1] for bravery but hate for it.

[1] There is a pun in the Chinese text of this paragraph that is impossible to bring out in English. When Motse said to the man " I have heard you are brave ", the Chinese words used also mean " I have heard, you admire bravery " 子 好 勇.

BOOK XII

CHAPTER XLVII

Esteem for Righteousness

Motse said : Of the multitude of things none is more valuable than righteousness. Suppose we say to a person : We shall give you a hat and shoes on condition you let us cut off your hands and feet. Would he agree to this ? Of course, he will not agree. Why ? Just because hats and shoes are not so valuable as hands and feet. Again (if we say), we shall give you the whole world on condition you let us kill you. Would he agree to this ? Of course he will not agree. Why ? Just because the world is not so valuable as one's person. Yet people have struggled against one another for a single principle. This shows righteousness is even more valuable than one's person. Hence we say, of the multitude of things none is more valuable than righteousness.

On his way from Lu to Ch'i, Motse met an old friend who said to him : "Nowadays none in the world practises any righteousness. You are merely inflicting pain on yourself by trying to practise righteousness. You had better give it up." Motse replied : Suppose a man has ten sons. Only one attends to the farm while the other nine stay at home. Then the farmer must work all the more vigorously. Why ? Because many eat while few work. Now, none in the world practises righteousness. Then you should all the more encourage me. Why do you stop me ?

Motse travelled south to Ch'u to see Lord Hui of Ch'u.
Lord Hui refused to see him with the excuse of his being old,
and let Mu Ho receive him. Motse talked to Mu Ho and
Mu Ho was greatly pleased. He said to Motse : " Your
idea may be quite good. But our Lord is a great Lord of the
empire. Can't he refuse to employ them because they come
only from a humble man ? " Motse replied : So long as they
are applicable they are like (good) medicines, which are only
the roots of herbs. Yet even the emperor takes them to
cure his sickness. Does he refuse to take them because they
are only the roots of a herb ? Now, the farmer pays his tax
to the superior. (With this,) the superior prepares wine
and cakes to do sacrifice to God, ghosts and spirits. Do these
refuse to accept them because they come from the humble ?
So, even a humble man can yet be compared to the farmer,
or, at least to medicine. Is he even of less value than the
roots of a herb ? Moreover, has not my Lord heard the story
of T'ang ? Anciently, T'ang was going to see Yi Yin and
let a son of the house of P'eng be the driver. On the way,
the son of P'eng inquired where the lord was going. T'ang
told him that he was going to see Yi Yin. The son of P'eng
said : " Yi Yin is but a humble man of the world. If you
want to see him just send for him and he will feel quite
flattered." T'ang said : " This is not what you can understand. Here is some medicine. When taken, it will sharpen
the ears and brighten the eyes. Then I shall be pleased and
endeavour to take it. Now, Yi Yin to me is like a
good physician and an effective medicine. Yet you don't
think I should see him. It means you do not want to see
me become good." Thereupon he dismissed the son of P'eng

and did not let him drive any more.   They did not resume
their journey till the son of P'eng became respectful.

Motse said : Any word, any action, that is beneficial
to Heaven, the spirits, and the people is to be carried out.
Any word, any action, that is harmful to Heaven, the spirits,
and the people is to be abandoned.   Any word, any action,
that is in harmony with the sage-kings of the Three Dynasties,
Yao, Shun, Yü, T'ang, Wen, and Wu, is to be carried out.
Any word, any action, that is in agreement with the wicked
kings of the Three Dynasties, Chieh, Chow, Yu, and Li, is
to be abandoned.

Motse said : Any principle that can modify conduct,
(expound) much ; any principle that cannot modify conduct,
do not (expound) much.   To (expound) much what cannot
modify conduct is just to wear out one's mouth.

Motse said : The six peculiarities must be removed.   When
silent one should be deliberating ; when talking one should
instruct ;   when acting one should achieve (something).
When one employs these three alternatively he will be a
sage.   Pleasure, anger, joy, sorrow, love (and hate) are to be
removed and magnanimity and righteousness are to replace
them.   When hands, feet, mouth, nose, ears (and eyes) are
employed for righteousness, then one will surely be a sage.

Motse said to a few of his disciples : Though one cannot
achieve righteousness one must not abandon the way, just
as the carpenter must not blame the line though he cannot
saw the lumber straight.

Motse said : As the gentlemen in the world cannot be
butchers of dogs and pigs, they would refuse when asked to
be such.   Yet, though they are not capable of being ministers

in a state, they would accept it when asked to be such.   Isn't
this perverse ?

Motse said :   The blind say that which is bright
is white, that which is dark is black.   Even the keen-
sighted cannot alter this.   But if we should mix up the
black and white objects and let the blind select them they
could not do it.   Hence the reason that I say the blind
do not know white from black does not lie in the matter of
definition but in the process of selection.   Now, the way
the gentlemen of the world define magnanimity even Yü
and T'ang cannot alter.   But when we mix up magnanimous
conduct with unmagnanimous conduct and let the gentlemen
of the world choose them they do not know which is which.
So, the reason that I say the gentlemen of the world do
not know magnanimity does not lie in the matter of definition
either ; it also lies in the process of selection.

Motse said : The gentlemen of to-day handle their persons
with even less care than the merchant would handle a bale
of cloth.   When the merchant handles a bale of cloth
he dare not sell it without discretion ; he will surely select
a good one.   But the gentlemen of to-day handle their persons
quite differently.   Whatever they happen to desire they will
carry out.   In the more severe cases they fall into punishment ; even in less severe cases they are visited with condemnation.   So then the gentlemen are even less careful
in handling their persons than the merchant is in handling
a bale of cloth.

Motse said : The gentlemen of our time desire to achieve
righteousness.   Yet when we endeavour to help them in
the cultivation of their personality they become resentful.

This is like desiring the completion of a wall and becoming resentful when helped in the building. Isn't this perverse ?

Motse said : The sage-kings of old wanted to have their teaching passed to future generations. Therefore they recorded it on bamboos and silk and engraved it in metal and stone to bequeath to posterity so that their descendants could follow it. Now the ways of the early kings are known but not carried out. This is to break the tradition of the early kings.

Motse brought numerous books in his wagon drawers on his southern journey as an envoy to Wei. Hsien T'angtse saw them and was surprised. He inquired : " Sir, you have instructed Kung Shang Kuo [1] just to consider the right and wrong (of any case), and do no more. Now you, sir, bring very many books along. What can be the use for them ? " Motse said : Anciently, Duke Tan of Chou read one hundred pages every morning and received seventy scholars every evening. Therefore his achievements as minister to the emperor have lasted till this day. I have no superior above me to serve, nor any farm below to attend to. How dare I neglect these (books) ? I have heard, though the (different) ways lead to the same end they are not presented without deviations. And the common people do not know how to place proper importance in what they hear. Hence the large number of books. When one has reviewed the ideas and has thought deeply on them then he understands the essentials which lead to the same end. Therefore he does not need to be instructed by books. Why should you feel so much surprised ?

---

[1] Kung Shang Kuo is a disciple of Motse.

Motse said to Kung Liang Huantse [1] : Wei is a small state situated between Ch'i and Chin.[2] It is like a poor family in the midst of rich families. For a poor family to imitate the rich families in the extravagance in clothing and food, ruin is assured. Now we find in your house hundreds of decorated vehicles, hundreds of horses fed on grain, several hundred women clothed with finery and embroidery. If the expenditures for the decorations of the vehicles, food to the horses, and the embroidered clothes are used to maintain soldiers, there should be more than a thousand. Upon emergency, several hundred of them can be stationed at the van and several hundred can be stationed in the rear. To do this or to let the several hundred women hold the van and the rear, which is more secure ? I should think to keep women is not so secure as to maintain soldiers.

Motse had introduced somebody to office in Wei. The man went and returned. Motse asked him why he returned. He answered: " In counsel my opinions were not considered. Being promised a thousand p'en [3] I was given only five hundred. Therefore I left." Motse inquired : Suppose you were given more than a thousand p'en, would you still leave ? It was answered, no. Motse said : Then it is not because of lack of consideration. It is because of the smallness of the salary.

Motse said : The gentlemen of the world have even less regard for the righteous man than for the grain carrier.

[1] Kung Liang Huantse is a minister of Wei.

[2] Cf. the Sketch-Map appended in *Motse, the Neglected Rival of Confucius.*

[3] A P'en 盆 is equal to thirteen Chinese bushels, tou 斗. It was the practice at the time to collect taxes and pay salaries all in kind.

If a carrier was resting by the road side and was unable to
rise up, the gentlemen would surely help him to rise upon
seeing him, whether he be old or young, honourable or humble.
Why ? Because it is right. But when the gentleman who
practises righteousness urges them with the way of the early
kings, they are not only unwilling to carry it out but will
even trample it down. So, then, the gentlemen of the world
have even less regard for the righteous man than for the
grain carrier.

Motse said : The merchants go everywhere to do business
and their gain is doubled and multiplied. They persist
notwithstanding the difficulties at the passes and bridges,
and the dangers of the highwaymen and robbers. Now the
gentlemen can sit down and teach righteousness. There
are no difficulties at the passes and bridges or dangers from
highwaymen and robbers. Their gain should be not only
doubled and multiplied but become incalculable. Yet,
they will not do it. Then the gentlemen are not as discerning as the merchants in their calculation of benefits.

Motse was going North to Ch'i and met a fortune teller
on the way. The fortune teller told him : " God kills the
black dragon in the North to-day. Now, your complexion
is dark. You must not go North." Motse did not listen to
him and went North. At the Tse River he could proceed
no further and returned. The fortune teller said : " I have
told you that you must not go North." Motse said : People
on the South, of course, cannot go North (of the Tse River),
but neither can those on the North come South. (Moreover),
there are the dark-complexioned, but there are also the
fair-complexioned. Why is it that neither can proceed ?

Besides, God kills the blue dragon on the days of Chia and of I [1] in the East, the red dragon on the days of Ping and of Ting [1] in the South, the white dragon on the days of Keng and of Hsin [1] in the West, and the black dragon on the days of Jen and of Kuei [1] in the North. According to you then all the travellers in the world will be prohibited,[2] then all their plans will be curbed and the world made empty. Your idea is not to be adopted.

Motse said : My principle is sufficient. To abandon my principle and exercise thought is like abandoning the crop and trying to pick up grains. To refute my principle with one's own principle is like throwing an egg against a boulder. The eggs in the world would be exhausted without doing any harm to the boulder.

[1] These characters are members in the Chinese Sexagenary Cycle. Briefly the Cycle consists of two series of characters. The Heavenly Stems number twelve. The Earthly Branches number ten. As 60 is the least common multiple of 12 and 10, we have the Cycle of Sixty. In ancient times as in that of Motse it was used to designate days. Later it was used both for months and years, and specially the latter. For a more detailed treatment of this point cf. James Legge : " On Chinese Chronology," paper read before the Victoria Institute, 1892.

[2] In the last sentence eight of the ten Earthly Branches are mentioned. Pi Yuan in his edition of the text added " and the yellow dragon on the days of Wu and of Chi in the middle." This addition seems to me to be plausible because it completes the five legendary dragons, and the statement in the text will then include all the days, as each day must have a Stem and a Branch for its name, and there will be more sense to this sentence.

CHAPTER XLVIII [1]

KUNG MENG

Kung Mengtse [2] said to Motse : " The gentleman should fold his hands on the breast in waiting. He will speak when consulted ; he will not speak when not consulted. He is like a bell ; when struck it sounds, when not struck it does not sound. Motse said : This idea covers three phases of which you know but one ; so you do not understand what you are talking about. In the case of the ruler's committing violence in the state, to go and warn him will be called insolence, and to offer warning through those around him will be called meddling with counsel. This is where the gentleman hesitates (to speak). Now, if the ruler, in his administration, meets with some difficulty in the state resembling a machine about to shoot, [3] . . . the gentleman must give warning. So the benefit to the ruler [3] . . . . In such cases although he is not asked he should give counsel. Again, if the lord should launch out on some unrighteous, extraordinary enterprise ; and if in possession of clever military schemes, he should attack innocent states with a view to extending his territory, collecting taxes and gathering wealth ; and if in taking such a course he meet with humiliation, as it is beneficial neither to the victor nor to the vanquished—and hence harmful to both—in such a

---

[1] This chapter contains mainly some more criticisms of Confucianism. The arguments are presented in dialogue form and are less formal and systematic.

[2] *Supra*, p. 218 and note 2 same page.

[3] Text incomplete.

case the gentleman must respond with counsel though he is not asked. Moreover, according to what you have said, the gentleman is to fold his hands on his breast and wait. He will speak when consulted ; he will not speak when not consulted. He is like a bell ; when struck it sounds, when not struck it does not sound. Now, none had asked you and yet you spoke. Is this what you call sounding without being struck ? Is this what you call ungentlemanly ?

Kung Mengtse said to Motse : " How is it possible for the people to be ignorant of what is really good ? For instance, when the able fortune teller remains at home and does not go abroad, he will have grain in abundance ; when the beautful maiden remains at home and does not go abroad, people will compete in obtaining her. On the other hand if she should set forth to sell herself, none would take her. Now you go about, trying to persuade everybody, wherefore all this fuss ? " Motse said : In the present world of chaos those who seek the beautiful maidens are many. So, though they remain at home most people would take them. But those who seek goodness are few. Without intelligent persuasion people will not understand. Moreover, suppose here are two people good at fortune telling. One travels about to tell people's fortunes, and the other remains at home and does not go abroad. Which of these two will have more grain ? Kung Mengtse said that he who travels about and tells people's fortunes will have more grain. Motse said : So with magnanimity and righteousness. He who travels about and urges the people has more merit also. Why not, then, let us travel about and urge the people ?

Kung Mengtse, wearing a ceremonial hat, carrying the

officials' tablet,[1] and in the cloak of the learned, came to
see Motse and asked : " Does the gentleman dress in appropriate attire before acting.   Or does he do his business first
and then consider his attire ? " Motse said : Action does
not depend on attire.   Kung Mengtse asked how is it possible
to know.   Motse said : Formerly, Lord Huan of Ch'i
(685–643 B.C.), wearing a high hat and a wide girdle, with
a gold sword and wooden shield, governed his state.   And
his state became orderly.   Lord Wen of Chin (780–746 B.C.),
wearing garments of coarse cloth and sheepskin cloak, with
the sword in a leather belt, governed his state.   And his state
became orderly.   Lord Chuang of Ch'u (671–626 B.C.),
wearing a gaudy hat with a tassel, and a red garment and a
big gown, governed his state.   And his state became orderly.
Lord Kou Chien of Yüeh (496–465 B.C.), had his hair cut short [2]
and his body tattooed and governed his state, and his state
became orderly.   Now, these four lords differed in attire
but agreed in action.   I therefore know action does not depend
on attire.   Kung Mengtse said : " That is fine.   I have heard
that it is unlucky to keep goodness in darkness.   So, let me
go and put away the tablet and change the hat and come
back to see you.   Is this all right ? " Motse said : Please
come out with your errand.   If you have to put away the
tablet and change the hat before you can see me, then, action
does depend on attire.

Kung Mengtse said : " The gentleman has to be ancient

---

[1] This tablet is called hu 笏. It is something quite similar to kuei
珪 both in shape and in function. For kuei, see p. 111, note 2.

[2] The Chinese then customarily let their hair grow and wound it up on the
top of their heads.

in attire and in speech before he can be magnanimous."
Motse said : In ancient times, minister Fei Chung of Emperor
Chow of Shang was the terror of the world. While Baron
Chi and Baron Wei were the sages of the world. Now these
spoke the same dialect, but the latter were magnanimous
and the former was wicked. (Later), Duke Tan of Chou was
the sage of the world and Uncle Kuan was the villain of the
world. Now these wore the same attire [1] but the former was
magnanimous and the latter wicked. Then, virtue evidently
does not depend on the antiquity of attire and speech. Moreover, you are following only Chou and not Hsia. Your
antiquity does not go back far enough.

Kung Mengtse said to Motse : "In ancient times, in assigning
ranks the sage-kings [2] crowned the most sagacious as emperor,
and appointed the others as ministers and secretaries.
Now Confucius had an extensive knowledge of poetry [3] and
history,[3] a clear understanding of ceremonials [3] and music,[3]
and an intimate insight into many things. If it fell upon
Confucius to be the sage-king, why should he not make
himself emperor ? " Motse said : The wise man should
reverence Heaven and worship the spirits, love the people
and economize in expenditures. Combining these we get
wisdom. Now, you say, Confucius had an extensive knowledge of poetry and history, a clear understanding of
ceremonials and music, and an intimate insight into many
things. Therefore, you think, he should be made emperor.

---

[1] Kuan and Tan were brothers and both were uncles of Emperor Ch'eng.
Naturally they had the same attire of royalty.

[2] The sense of " sage-king " here seems to denote a disinterested judge
of merits selecting rulers for the people.

[3] These were the departments of the Classics.

This is like estimating one's wealth by counting the number of notches.[1]

Kung Mengtse said: "Poverty or wealth, old age or untimely death, all are determined by Heaven and they cannot be altered." Again, he said: "The superior man must learn." Motse said: To hold fatalism and teach people to learn is like telling him to cover his hair and yet remove his hat.

Kung Mengtse said to Motse: "There is only righteousness and unrighteousness, but no such thing as propitiousness or unpropitiousness." Motse said: The ancient sage-kings all regarded the ghosts and spirits as intelligent and in control of calamity and blessing. They held there was propitiousness and unpropitiousness and thereby the government was well administered and the country was secure. From Chieh and Chow down they all regarded the ghosts and spirits as unintelligent and not in control of calamity and blessing. They held there was no propitiousness and unpropitiousness, and thereby the government became disorderly and the country in danger. So, the book of the ancient kings "Chitse"[2] says, "Pride brings calamity." That is to say, the evil act will be punished and the good act will be rewarded.

Motse said to Kung Mengtse: According to the ceremonial,

---

[1] Contracts for loans were then made on bamboos. The creditor and the debtor were to hold a piece each. And the number of notches cut on the edges is the mark of identification. The story tells of a man of Sung who while travelling picked up one part of a contract. He was pleased and went home and counted the number of notches to find out how rich he was.

[2] Apparently a lost essay in *Shu Ching* named after Chitse. Chitse is referred to in an earlier paragraph in this chapter as Baron Chi, p. 233.

for the death of the ruler, the parents, the wife, and the first-born son, there shall be mourning for three years. For the elder uncle, younger uncle, elder brother, younger brother, and first cousins within the family, five months. And for the aunt, the sister, the uncle on mother's side, and the nephew on sister's side, there will be mourning of several months for each. Many also use the intervals between periods of mourning to read the Three Hundred Poems according to rhymes, to play them on the string instruments,[1] to sing them, and to dance to them.[2] If your counsel should be followed when can the gentleman attend to government, the common man to work ? Kung Mengtse said : " When the country is in chaos it should be put in order ; when it is in order, ceremonials and music may be pursued. When the country is poor work should be attended to ; when it is rich, ceremonials and music may be pursued." Motse said : A country may be orderly. But it is because it is being well governed that it is orderly. As soon as good administration is abandoned, order disappears also. A country may be rich. But it is because work is being attended to that it is rich. As soon as work is abandoned, wealth disappears also. Therefore although a country is orderly it is necessary to encourage unceasing attention to administration. Now, you say, when the country is in order, ceremonials and music may be pursued. But put it in order when it becomes disorderly. This is similar to digging a well when some one is choked

[1] The string instruments are namely, ch'in and she. *Supra*, p. 175, and note 1 same page.

[2] This seems to be similar to the dancing interpretation of classical compositions in the West. Evidently the departments of poetry, music, and dancing were not marked out very clearly.

and to seeking a physician when some one is dead. In ancient times, the wicked kings of the Three Dynasties, Chieh, Chow, Yu, and Li, revelled in music, and did not remember their people. Therefore they suffered capital punishment and brought calamity to their empire. And it was all from following this idea.

Kung Mengtse said that there were no ghosts and spirits; again, he said that the superior man must learn sacrifice and worship. Motse said: To hold there are no spirits and learn sacrificial ceremonials is comparable to learning the ceremonials of hospitality while there is no guest or to making fishing nets while there are no fish.

Kung Mengtse said to Motse: "You think mourning for three years is wrong. Your mourning for three days is also wrong." Motse replied: You hold mourning for three years and condemn mourning for three days. This is similar to the naked person condemning the person who lifted up his garments for indecency.

Kung Mengtse asked Motse whether it is wisdom when one knows something better than some other person. Motse answered: A fool may know something better than some other person. Yet can the fool be said to be wise?

Kung Mengtse said: "I mourn for three years in imitation of the affection that my son shows to his parents." Motse said: But does the baby have an intelligence to love only its parents? Why, then, should it keep on crying when the parents are not to be had? [1] It is really the extreme

---

[1] The theory in modern social psychology that the baby's love for its parents is due to conditioned response may easily be grafted here to Motse's scepticism about native intelligence. But we must be cautious to say that he really meant this.

degree of foolishness. Thus, is the intelligence of the Confucianists any higher than that of the baby ?

Motse asked a Confucianist why the Confucianists pursued music. He replied, music is pursued for music's sake. Motse said : You have not yet answered me. Suppose I asked, why build houses. And you answered, it is to keep off the cold in winter, and the heat in summer, and to separate men from women. Then you would have told me the reason for building houses. Now I am asking why pursue music. And you answer music is pursued for music's sake. This is comparable to : " Why build houses ? " " Houses are built for houses' sakes."

Motse said to Ch'engtse [1] : In the teaching of the Confucianists there are four principles sufficient to ruin the empire : The Confucianists hold Heaven is unintelligent, and the ghosts are inanimate. Heaven and spirits are displeased. This is sufficient to ruin the world. Again they (practise) elaborate funerals and extended mourning. They use several inner and outer coffins, and many pieces of shrouds. The funeral procession looks like house-moving. Crying and weeping last three years. They cannot stand up without support and cannot walk without a cane. Their ears cannot hear and their eyes cannot see. This is sufficient to ruin the world. And they play the string instruments and dance and sing and practise songs and music. This is sufficient to ruin the empire. And, finally, they suppose there is fate and that poverty or wealth, old age or untimely death, order or chaos, security or danger, are all predetermined and cannot be altered. Applying this belief, those in authority,

---

[1] Ch'engtse or Ch'eng Fan is another Confucianist.

of course, will not attend to government and those below will not attend to work. Again, this is sufficient to ruin the world. Ch'engtse said : " Sir, you are accusing the Confucianists of too much." Motse said : If the Confucianists hold nothing like these four principles and yet I say they do then it is false accusation. Now that the Confucianists do hold these four principles and I say so, then it is not accusation but information.

Ch'engtse had nothing more to say and went out. Motse called him back. After being seated he continued : " What you, sir, have just said is not without fault. For according to what you have said, there will be no praise of Yü or blame of Chieh and Chow." Motse replied : Not at all. You are only cleverly criticizing me according to traditional notions. When attack is heavy defence must be strong. When attack is light defence must be light. To criticize according to traditional notions is similar to trying to kill a moth with a thill.

In a discussion with Ch'engtse, Motse cited Confucius. Ch'engtse inquired why, since he condemned Confucianism, he cited Confucius. Motse said : This has reference to what is right and cannot be altered. When the bird becomes aware of the danger of heat and of drought, it flies high. When the fish becomes aware of the danger of heat and of drought, it swims low. In such circumstances even the deliberations of Yü and T'ang cannot differ from this. The bird and the fish may be said to be unintelligent. Yet, in some instances, even Yü and T'ang would follow them. Should I never cite Confucius ?

A man visited Motse's school. He was physically well

built and mentally brilliant. Desiring to have him in his school, Motse told him to come and study and that he would make him an official. Persuaded by such an attractive promise, he came to study. In a year, he demanded a position of Motse. Motse said : I have not made you an official. But have you not heard the story of Lu ? There were five brothers in Lu whose father passed away. The eldest son loved wine and would not conduct the funeral. The four younger brothers said to him, " You conduct the funeral for us, and we shall buy wine for you." He was persuaded by such an attractive promise and buried (his father). After the burial he demanded wine of the four brothers. The four brothers told him, " We will not give you any wine. You are to bury your father and we, ours. Is your father only ours ? If you don't bury him people will laugh at you, therefore we urged you to bury him." Now, you have done right and I have done right, is it only my righteousness ? If you don't learn, people will laugh at you. Therefore I urged you to learn.

A man visited Motse's school. Motse said : Why not come and study ? Came the reply, " None of my family is learned." Motse said : No matter. Does he who loves beauty say, none of my family loves it, therefore I will not ? And does he who desires wealth and honour say, none of my family desires them, therefore I will not ? Now, in the love of beauty and desire for wealth and honour, one goes ahead regardless of others. And righteousness is the greatest thing in the world. Why should one follow others in doing it ?

A man visited Motse's school and said to Motse : " Sir, you teach that the ghosts and spirits are intelligent and can bring calamity or blessing to man. They will enrich the good and harm the evil. Now, I have served you for a long time. Yet no blessing has come. Can it be that your teaching is not entirely correct, and that the ghosts and spirits are not intelligent? Else why don't I obtain any blessing?" Motse said: Though you have not obtained any blessing, how does that invalidate my teaching and how does that make the ghosts and spirits unintelligent? He replied that he did not know. Motse continued: Suppose there is a man ten times as virtuous as you are, can you praise him ten times while you praise yourself but once? He answered that he could not. Now suppose there is a man a hundred times as virtuous as you are, can you during your whole life praise him and not praise yourself even once? He answered that he could not. Motse said: He who obscured the virtues of one person is guilty. Now, you have obscured the virtues of so many. You must be guilty of very much. Wherewith can you expect blessing?

Motse was sick. Tieh Pi came and inquired: "Sir, you have taught the ghosts and spirits are intelligent and are in control of calamity and blessing. They will reward the good and punish the evil. Now you are a sage. How can you become sick? Can it be that your teaching was not entirely correct, that the ghosts and spirits are after all unintelligent? Motse said: Though I am sick how (does it follow that the ghosts and spirits) should be unintelligent? There are many ways by which a man can contract diseases. Some are affected by climate, some by fatigue. If there are a hundred gates and only one of them is closed, how is it that the burglar should not be able to get in?

Some of the pupils asked to learn archery with Motse. Motse said : Impossible. The wise should measure how far his energy can go and plan his career accordingly. Even a soldier cannot fight and help somebody at the same time. Now you are no soldiers. How can you be both accomplished scholars and accomplished archers ?

Some of the pupils reported to Motse that Kaotse [1] proclaimed Motse to be teaching righteousness but doing wickedness, and urged him to denounce Kaotse. Motse said : That would not do. To praise my teaching and blame my conduct is yet better than indifference. Suppose there is some one who declares that Ti [2] is quite unmagnanimous, that he reverences Heaven, worships spirits, and loves men— this is yet better than indifference. Now, Kaotse was quite discriminating in his statements. He does not blame me for teaching magnanimity and righteousness. So, blame from Kaotse is yet better than indifference.

Some of the pupils reported to Motse that Kaotse was zealous in practising magnanimity. Motse remarked : It may not really be so at all. Kaotse practises magnanimity in the same way as the man who stands on his tip toe to appear tall and spreads himself to appear broad. It cannot last long.

---

[1] There is a Book in *Mencius* 孟 子 named " Kaotse ", Legge, vol. ii, bk. vi, pp. 270–324. Kaotse there was the advocate of the morally indifferent character of original human nature, engaged in a controversy with Mencius who taught natural goodness. He is said to have once been a pupil of Mencius. If this is true, the Kaotse here mentioned must be a different person. But considering that Motse probably died about 390 B.C., and that Mencius was born 372 B.C., it is not impossible for the same person to have held conversations with both Motse and Mencius.

[2] Here Motse is referring to himself by name.

Kaotse said to Motse that he can administer the country and the government. Motse said : To govern is to carry out what one teaches. Now you don't behave according to what you teach, this means that you yourself are in revolt. Being unable to govern one's self, how can one govern the country ? Your self will set it in chaos.

BOOK XIII

CHAPTER XLIX

LU'S QUESTION

The Lord of Lu asked Motse: " I fear Ch'i will attack me.
Is there any remedy ? " Motse said : Yes, the sage-kings
of the Three Dynasties, Yü, T'ang, Wen, and Wu, were
originally feudal lords of states of only a hundred li square.
Yet, enlisting the loyal and practising righteousness, they
acquired the empire. While the wicked kings of the Three
Dynasties, Chieh, Chow, Yu, and Li, by estranging the loyal
and practising wickedness, lost the empire. I wish your
Lordship would reverence Heaven and the spirits above and
love and benefit the people below ; prepare plenty of furs
and money and humble your speech to befriend all the
neighbouring lords, and lead the state to serve Ch'i. Besides
this, indeed nothing can be done.

Ch'i was going to attack Lu. Motse said to Hsiang Tse
Niu [1] : To attack Lu is a great wrong on the part of Ch'i.
Formerly, the Lord of Wu attacked Yüeh on the east and drove
(Lord Kou Chien of Yüeh) to take refuge upon Kuei Chi.[2] He
attacked Ch'u on the west and held fast Lord Chao at Sui.
On the north he attacked Ch'i and brought Kuotse [3] back
to Wu. The feudal lords then took vengeance and his people

---

[1] Hsiang Tse Niu is a general of Ch'i.

[2] Kuei Chi is the name of a hill.

[3] Kuotse is also a general of Ch'i. His name is Kuo Shu. But the two
words " kuo tse " 國 子 might also mean the Prince of the state. Forke,
for instance, adopted the latter reading in his translation.

complained of the hardship and would not be commanded. Thereupon the state perished and the Lord of Wu was executed. Formerly, Chih Po attacked both the house of Fan and the house of Chung Hsing, and absorbed all the land of the Three Chin states. The feudal lords then took vengeance and his people complained of the hardship and would not be commanded. Thereupon the state perished and he was executed. Therefore the attack of a large state on a small state is injury to both and the consequences of the wrong will always return to the large state.

Motse saw the Grand Lord of Ch'i and said : Suppose here is a sword. When it is tried on a man's neck it severs it swiftly. Can it be said to be sharp ? The Grand Lord said it is sharp. Motse said : When it is tried on several men's necks, it severs them swiftly. Can it be said to be sharp ? The Grand Lord said it is sharp. Motse said : Of course, the sword is (proved to be) sharp, but who will take the curse of the deed upon him ? [1] The Grand Lord said that the sword reaped the benefit but he who tries it will be visited by the curse for the act. Motse continued : Now to capture a state, ruin an army, and destroy the people—who will be visited by the curse for this act ? The Grand Lord looked down and up and deliberated, saying : " I shall be visited with the curse for this act."

Prince Wen of Lu Yang was going to attack Cheng. Motse heard of it and tried to stop him, saying to him : Suppose within the borders of Lu Yang the large cities should attack the

[1] There is a play upon words in this paragraph in the Chinese text, which disappears in the translation. The word used for " sharp " is " li " 利, which means also " benefit ". And it is as the opposite to the latter meaning of the word that the idea of " curse " is brought in.

small cities and the large houses attack the small houses, killing the people and carrying away the oxen and horses, dogs and hogs, cloth and silk, and grains and valuables. What would you say ? Prince Wen of Lu Yang replied : " Within the borders of Lu Yang all are my subjects. Now, should the large cities attack the small cities and the large houses attack the small houses, carrying away their valuables, I should punish them severely." Motse said : Now, Heaven possesses the whole world just as your Lordship possesses your state. But you are raising an army to attack Cheng. Shouldn't punishment from Heaven come to you ?

Prince Wen of Lu Yang said : " Why should you, sir, prevent me from attacking Cheng ? I attack Cheng in accordance with the will of Heaven. The people of Cheng have murdered their father [1] for three generations. Heaven has been visiting them with punishment. It has caused them to be unprosperous for three years. I am only helping Heaven to carry out the punishment." Motse said : The people of Cheng have murdered their father for three genera-tions. Heaven has been visiting them with punishment. It has caused them to be unprosperous for three years. The punishment of Heaven is sufficient. Yet, you are raising an army to attack Cheng, proclaiming : " My attack on Cheng is in accordance with the will of Heaven." Suppose there is a man whose son is strong but insolent. So the father punished him with a ferule. But the neighbour's father struck him with a heavy staff, saying : " It is in

---

[1] " Father " here refers to the lord. Among the five cardinal relations that between the lord and the minister comes first and that between the father and the son second.

accordance with his father's will that I strike him.'' Isn't
this perversity ?

Motse said to Prince Wen of Lu Yang : If a lord had
attacked the neighbouring states, killed their people, carried
away their oxen and horses, grains and valuables, a lord
might yet record it on bamboos and silk and engrave it on
metal and stone and write it up into maxims on the bell
and the ting to hand down to posterity, saying : " None
possess so much as I.'' Now, the unscrupulous common
man also attacks neighbouring homes, kills their inmates,
and takes the dogs and hogs, food and clothing. They would
also like to record it on bamboos and silk and write it up into
maxims on the vessels and dishes to hand down to posterity,
saying : " None possesses so much as I.'' Is this permissible ?
Prince Wen of Lu Yang said : "According to what you have
said then what the world takes for granted may not be right
after all.''

Motse said to Prince Wen of Lu Yang : The gentlemen of
the world know only trifles but not things of importance.
If a man steals a dog or pig, they call him wicked. But
stealing a state or a city is regarded as righteous. This
is similar to calling it white when one sees a little white, but
calling it black when he sees much white. And this is what
is meant when we say the gentlemen of the world know only
trifles and not things of importance.

Prince Wen of Lu Yang said to Motse : " There is a cannibal
tribe on the south of Ch'u.[1] When the first son is born

---

[1] The same tribe was mentioned in another connexion on p. 133. This
point needs to be made, as in the Chinese text the name there given is 炎
and not 啖 as is given here, and is liable to mis-reading. Evidently they
refer to the same tribe.

they dissect and devour him. This is said to be propitious to his younger brothers. If he tastes delicious, he will be offered to the chief, and if the chief is pleased the father will be rewarded. Isn't this a wicked custom?" Motse said : So is the custom in China. How is killing the father and rewarding the son different from devouring the son and rewarding the father? If magnanimity and righteousness are not observed, wherefore shall we condemn the barbarians for eating their sons?

Upon the death of a favourite concubine of the Lord of Lu, somebody in Lu wrote an obituary for her. The Lord of Lu was pleased with it and employed the writer. Motse heard of it and remarked : An obituary is but to narrate the ambitions of the dead. To employ the man because his obituary is pleasing is like making the wild cat pull a carriage.

Prince Wen of Lu Yang asked Motse : " Suppose somebody was recommended as a loyal minister. And he would bow down when I let him bow down ; he would bend back when I let him bend back. Staying there he would be silent, and when called upon he would answer. Can this be said to be loyal?" Motse said : To bow down when permitted, to bend back when permitted—this is but a shadow. To remain silent when let alone, to answer when called upon— this is but an echo. What would your Lordship get out of an echo or a shadow? According to my conception of a loyal minister, when the superior is at fault he should wait and warn ; possessing a good idea he should give counsel to the superior without revealing it to the world ; he should correct irregularities and lead in goodness ; he should identify himself with the superior and not ally himself with subordinates. So that goodness and excellences will be attributed to the superior and complaints and grudges lodged against the subordinates ; so that ease and happiness be with the superior and trouble and worry with the ministers. This is what I call a loyal minister.

The Lord of Lu consulted Motse, saying : " Now I have two sons. One likes learning and the other likes dividing property for people. Which one should be crowned Prince ? " Motse said : We can't tell (just from this). It may be that they behave so just for the praise and reward of it. The fisherman's bait is not intended to feed the fish. Trapping a mouse with worms is not for the love of the mouse. I wish your Lordship would observe both their intention and consequences.

There was a man in Lu who sent his son to Motse to study. The son perished in a battle. The father blamed Motse for it. Motse said : You wanted to have your son trained. Now he had completed his training and died in battle. And you become sore. This is like trying to sell something, and yet becoming sore when it is sold. Isn't this peculiar ?

Among the rustic people living south of Lu there was a man by the name of Wu Lü. Making pottery in winter and farming in summer, he compared himself to Shun. Motse heard of him and went to see him. Wu Lü told Motse : " Righteousness is just righteousness. Wherefore all the verbosity ? " Moste asked him : Now, does what you call righteousness possess power to serve other people and produce wealth to divide among the people ? Wu Lü said that it does. Motse continued : I have deliberated about this matter. I have thought of becoming a farmer and feeding the people in

the world. If that could be successful I would become one.
But when a farmer's produce is divided among the world,
each person cannot get even one sheng of grain. Even if
he can obtain that much, evidently that cannot feed all
the hungry in the world. I have thought of becoming
a weaver and clothing all the people in the world. If
that could be successful I would become one. But when
a weaver's goods are divided among the world, each person
cannot get even a foot of cloth. Even if he can obtain that
much, evidently that cannot keep all who are cold in the
world warm. I have thought of putting on an armour and
carrying a weapon to come to the feudal lord's rescue. If
that could be successful I would become a soldier. Now
it is evident that a soldier cannot hold out against a regular
army. I concluded that none of these is as good as to
familiarize myself with the Tao of the ancient sage-kings,
and discover their principles, and to understand the word
of the sages and be clear about their expressions; and with
these to persuade the rulers and then the common people
and the pedestrians. When the rulers adopt my principles
their states will be orderly. When the common people and
the pedestrians adopt my principles their conduct will be
regulated. Therefore I think though I do not plow and feed
the hungry or weave and clothe the cold, I have greater
merit than those who plow and feed, and weave and clothe.
Therefore I think my merit is greater than that of those
who plow and weave though I do not do so.

Wu Lü kept on saying, "Righteousness is just righteousness. Wherefore all the verbosity?" Motse continued:
Suppose the world does not know how to plow. Who has

more merit, the man who teaches people to plow, or he who does not teach people to plow but simply plows himself? Wu Lü answered that he that teaches others to plow deserves more merit. Motse said: In the attack of an unrighteous state, does he that beats the drum and urges the soldiers to fight on, or does he that does not beat the drum and urge the soldiers to fight on but only fights on himself deserve more merit? Wu Lü said that he that beats the drum and urges the soldiers to fight on deserves more merit. Motse continued: Now the common people and the pedestrians in the world know little about righteousness. Naturally those who teach them righteousness deserve more merit too. Why don't you say so (in this case)? Would not my righteousness be advanced if I can encourage them in righteousness?

After Motse had paid Kung Shang Kuo a visit, Kung Shang Kuo recommended him to the Lord of Yüeh. The Lord of Yüeh was greatly pleased, saying to Kung Shang Kuo: "Sir, if you can induce Motse to come to Yüeh and instruct me I shall offer him five hundred li square of the land lying in the former state of Wu." Kung Shang Kuo promised to try and so fifty wagons were made ready to go to Lu and welcome Motse. (Kung Shang Kuo) told him: "When I tried to presuade the Lord of Yüeh with your principles he was quite pleased and said to me that if I could induce you to come to Yüeh and instruct him, he would offer you five hundred li square of the land lying in the former state of Wu." Motse said to Kung Shang Kuo: As you observe it, what is the intention of the Lord of Yüeh? If the Lord of Yüeh will listen to my word and adopt my way,

I shall come, asking only for food according to the capacity of my stomach, and clothing according to the stature of my body. I shall just be one of the ministers. What is the use of any commission ? On the other hand, if the Lord of Yüeh will not listen to my word and adopt my way and I should go nevertheless, I should then be selling my righteousness. As for selling righteousness I could very well do it in China, why should I then go out to Yüeh ? [1]

Motse was visiting Wei Yüeh.[2] The latter asked : " Now that you have seen the gentlemen of the four quarters, what would you say is the most urgent enterprise ? " Motse replied : Upon entering a country one should locate the need and work on that. If the country is upset in confusion, teach them with the (doctrines of) Exaltation of the Virtuous and Identification with the Superior. If the country is in poverty, teach them with Economy of Expenditures and Simplicity in Funeral. If the country is indulging in music and wine, teach them with Condemnation of Music and Anti-fatalism. If the country is insolent and without propriety, teach them to reverence Heaven and worship the spirits.[3] If the country is engaged in conquest and oppression, teach them with Universal Love and Condemnation of Offensive War. Hence we say, one should locate the need and work on that.

Motse had recommended Ts'ao Kungtse to Sung. He

---

[1] Yüeh was on the southern border of China. It was of barbarian origin, too. Cf. the Sketch Map appended in *Motse, the Neglected Rival of Confucius*.

[2] Wei Yüeh is a disciple of Motse.

[3] This, of course, refers to the two doctrines expounded in the Chapters on " Will of Heaven " and " On Ghost ".

returned in three years and saw Motse, saying : " When I first came to your school I had to wear short jackets and eat vegetable soup. Even this I could not have in the evening if I had had it in the morning. And I had nothing to offer and sacrifice to the ghosts and spirits. Now, on your account my family has become better off. And I could respectfully offer sacrifice and worship ghosts and spirits at home. Yet several members of my household died off, the six animals do not breed, and I have myself been troubled with ailments. I doubt if your way is after all to be adopted." Motse said : This is not fair. For what the ghosts and spirits desire of man is that when in high rank and receiving much emolument, he give up his position in favour of the virtuous ; that when possessing much wealth he share it with the poor. How can the ghosts and spirits merely desire to snatch food and drink ? [1] Now, when in high rank and receiving much emolument you did not give up your position in favour of the virtuous. This is your first step to bad fortune. Possessing much wealth you did not share it with the poor. This is your second step towards misfortune. Now you serve the ghosts and spirits by merely offering them sacrifice ; and you wonder whence come all the ailments. This is like shutting one out of a hundred gates and wondering whence the thieves entered. How can you invoke ghosts and spirits for blessing like this ?

The master of sacrifice of Lu offered one pig and asked for a hundred blessings. Upon hearing of it Motse said : This cannot be done. To give others little but to expect much from others would make them afraid of gifts. Now

---

[1] This refers to material offerings.

one pig is offered and a hundred blessings are asked of the
ghosts and spirits.   They would be quite afraid of a sacrifice
of oxen and sheep.   Anciently, when the sage-kings
worshipped the ghosts and spirits, they just offered them
sacrifice and that was all.   One would be better off to remain
poor than become rich by offering a pig for sacrifice and
asking for a hundred blessings.

P'eng Ch'ing Shengtse [1] said : " The past can be known,
the future cannot.'' Motse said : Suppose your parents
met with misfortune a hundred li away.   And there was
just the margin of a single day. If they could be reached
they would live, if not they would die.   Here are a strong
wagon and an excellent horse, and also a bad horse and a
square-wheeled cart.   And you are allowed to choose.   Which
would you take ?   It was replied that the excellent horse and
the strong wagon would of course make for a more speedy
journey. Motse said : How then is the future not knowable ? [2]

Meng Shan [3] praised Prince Tse Lü, saying : " Formerly,
in the uprising of Po Kung, Prince Tse Lü was held captive.
With axes around his waist and spears pointing at his heart,
Po Kung told him to be Lord and live or refuse and die.
Prince Tse Lü said to him, ' What an insult to me.   You
have killed my parents and now bait me with the state of
Ch'u.   If it is not righteous I would not even take the whole
empire, to say nothing of the state of Ch'u.'   Thus he refused. [4]

---

[1] Peng Ch'ing Shengtse is perhaps also a disciple of Motse.

[2] The Chinese text here is not so clear and definite. But this seems to be
the idea of the concluding question.

[3] Meng Shan is a follower of Motse.

[4] According to Tso Ch'iu Ming's " Commentary of Spring and Autumn ",
or Tso Chuan 左 傳, the Prince thereupon lost his life.

Wasn't Prince Tse Lü magnanimous ? " Motse said :
What he did was indeed difficult, but hardly magnanimous.
If he thought the Lord had gone astray from the Tao, why
not accept the offer and undertake the government himself ?
If he thought Po Kung was unrighteous, why not accept
the Lordship also, execute Po Kung, and then return the
Lordship to the Lord ? Therefore I say what he did was indeed
difficult, but hardly magnanimous.

Motse sent Sheng Cho [1] to serve Hsiang Tse Niu. Hsiang
Tse Niu invaded Lu three times, and Sheng Cho was three
times with him. Hearing of this, Motse sent Kao Suntse to
call him back, saying : I sent Cho there in order to cure
pride and regulate insolence. Now, Cho draws a large salary
and flatters his master. His master invaded Lu three times
and he was with him every time. This is like whipping
a horse by its martingale.[2] I have heard that to preach
righteousness but do it not is intentional commitment of
wrong. It is not that Cho is ignorant. It is a case of victory
of emolument over righteousness.

Formerly the people of Ch'u and the people of Yüeh had
a battle on the River.[3] The people of Ch'u were with the
stream in their advance but against it in their retreat. When
success was in sight they advanced. But when defeat was
confronting them they found it very difficult to retreat. On
the contrary the people of Yüeh advanced upstream but
retreated downstream. When success was in sight they would

---

[1] Sheng Cho, a follower of Motse.

[2] This is a figure meaning that instead of urging the man forward it puts
a stop to his advance, in virtue, of course.

[3] The Yangtse River is often called " the River " in China.

advance. And when defeat was confronting them they could easily retreat.[1]

With this advantage the people of Yüeh greatly defeated the people of Ch'u. Kung Shutse [2] came south from Lu to Ch'u, and began making implements for naval warfare which consisted of grappling hooks and rams. When the enemy were retreating they used the hooks. And when the enemy were advancing they employed the rams. And the weapons were made according to the length of these hooks and rams. The weapons of Ch'u thus were all standardized, and those of Yüeh were not. And, with this advantage, the people of Ch'u greatly defeated the people of Yüeh. Kung Shutse was proud of his cleverness and asked Motse: "There are the implements for grappling and ramming in my boats of war. Do you have such a device in your righteousness?" Motse said: The grappling and ramming device in my righteousness is more excellent than your implements in the boats of war. In my scheme, I pull with love and push with respect. If you do not pull with love there can be no intimacy. If you do not push with respect there will be rapid desecration. And desecration without real intimacy will soon end in separation. Therefore mutual love and mutual respect mean really mutual benefit. Now you pull people up to stop their retreat, but they would also pull you up and stop your retreat. You push people back to stop their advance, but they would also push you back to stop your advance. The mutual pulling and pushing are

---

[1] For the geographical situation of these two states consult the Sketch Map appended in *Motse, the Neglected Rival of Confucius*.

[2] Kung Shu Pan is a mechanical inventor of renown of the time.

just mutual injury. Therefore the device of pulling and pushing in my righteousness is more excellent than the implements of pulling and pushing in your boats of war.

Kung Shutse constructed a bird from bamboo and wood and when it was completed he flew it. It stayed up (in the air) for three days.[1] Kung Shutse was proud of his supreme skill. Motse said to him: Your accomplishment in constructing a bird does not compare with that of the carpenter in making a linch-pin. In a short while he could cut out the piece of wood of three inches. Yet it would carry a load of fifty shih.[2] For, any achievement that is beneficial to man is to be said to be skilful, and anything not beneficial is said to be clumsy.

Kung Shutse confessed to Motse: "Before I saw you, I wished to take Sung. Since I have seen you, even if Sung were offered me I would not take it if it is unrighteous." Motse said: Before you saw me you wished to take Sung. Since you have seen me even if Sung were offered you you would not take it if it is unrighteous. This means, I have given you Sung. If you engage yourself in doing righteousness, I shall yet give you the whole world.[3]

---

[1] This short passage has sometimes been referred to as a record of invention of the flying machine by the Chinese.

[2] One shih 石 = 120 chin 斤 ; the latter is equal to 1⅓ lb.

[3] This paragraph comes more properly at the end of the next chapter. At any rate the reference is to that event.

CHAPTER L

Kung Shu

Kung Shu Pan had completed the construction of Cloud-ladders for Ch'u and was going to attack Sung with them. Motse heard of it and set out from Ch'i. He walked ten days and ten nights [1] and arrived at Ying.[2] He saw Kung Shu Pan. The latter asked him what he wanted of him. Motse said: Some one in the north has humiliated me. I would like to have you kill him. Kung Shu Pan was displeased. Motse persisted, offering him ten chin.[3] Finally Kung Shu Pan said: "My principle is incompatible with murdering people."

Thereupon Motse rose and bowed twice [4] and spoke: Now, let me explain myself. While in the north I heard you were building ladders to attack Sung. Now, of what is Sung guilty? The state of Ching [5] has land to spare but is short of people. To destroy what is scarce in order to strive for what is already plenty cannot be said to be wise. Since Sung is innocent, to attack it cannot be said to be magnanimous. To fail to make an effort according to what you know cannot be said to be loyal. To make the effort without obtaining (the desired result) cannot be said to be effective. To hold a principle that forbids the killing of

[1] The same tale is told in some other works. It was said that Motse had to tear off parts of his garment to wrap up his feet for this continuous long walk.

[2] Ying is the capital of Ch'u, in what is now called Hupei Province.

[3] *Supra*, p. 214, note 2.

[4] This is an expression of apology.

[5] Ching and Ch'u are two names for the same state.

few but allows that of many cannot be said to be understanding the fundamental categories.

Kung Shu Pan became convinced. Motse urged further : Then why would you not stop it ? Kung Shu Pan said that could not be done as he had already promised the Lord. Motse said : Why not then present me to the Lord ? Kung Shu Pan agreed.

Motse saw the Lord and said : Suppose there is a man who, putting aside his elegant carriage, desires to steal his neighbour's shattered sedan ; putting aside his embroidery and finery, desires to steal his neighbour's short jacket ; putting aside his meat and grains desires to steal his neighbour's husks. What kind of a man would this be ? The Lord said that he must be suffering from kleptomania. Motse continued : The land of Ching amounts to five thousand li square while that of Sung is only five hundred, this is similar to the contrast between the elegant carriage and the shattered sedan. Ching possesses Yun Meng which is full of rhinoceroses and deer. The fish, tortoises and crocodiles in the Yangtse and the Han Rivers are the richest in the empire. While Sung is said to possess not even pheasants, rabbits, or foxes. This is similar to the contrast between meat and grains and husks. In Ching there are tall pines, spruces, cedars, and camphor trees. While Sung has no tall trees at all. This is similar to the contrast between embroidery and finery and the short jacket. When your ministers and generals set out to attack Sung, it seems to me there is the same analogy. I can see, my Lord, you will be violating righteousness to no advantage.

The Lord said : " That is all very well. But Kung Shu

Pan has already constructed the Cloud-ladders for me, and I must capture Sung." And he turned to Kung Shu Pan.

Motse untied his belt and laid out a city with it, and used a small stick for weapon. Kung Shu Pan set up nine different machines of attack. Motse repulsed him nine times. Kung Shu Pan was at an end with his machines of attack while Motse was far from being exhausted in defence.

Kung Shu Pan felt embarrassed and declared : " I know how I can put you down, but I would not tell." Motse also said : " I know how you can put me down, but I would not tell." The Lord of Ch'u asked what it was. Motse replied : Kung Shutse's idea is just to have me murdered. (Apparently) when I was murdered, Sung would be powerless at defence. And she would be subject to your attack. However, my disciples Ch'in Hua Li and others numbering three hundred are already armed with my implements of defence waiting on the city wall of Sung for the bandits from Ch'u. Though I be murdered, you cannot exhaust (the defence of Sung). The Lord of Ch'u said : " Well, then let us not attack Sung any more."

On his way back,[1] Motse passed through Sung. It was raining and he sought shelter in a pass. But the guard of the pass would not let him in. Thus it is said : " The merit of the man who cultivates himself before the spirits [2] is not recognized by the multitude. On the other hand, he who strives in the open is recognized."

---

[1] Back to Ch'i or Lu. Cf. discussion on this point in *Motse, the Neglected Rival of Confucius*, chap. ii.

[2] That is, in the dark, in secrecy.

INDEX